THE FLORIDA GUIDE TO POLITICAL APPOINTMENTS

ELIZABETH MCCALLLUM

Manufactured in the United States of America

@2003 Elizabeth McCallum

Published by Hill House Books
Brandon, Florida 33511-8113

McCallum, Elizabeth.
   The Florida guide to political appointments / by
Elizabeth McCallum.
    p. cm.
   Includes index.
   LCCN 2003104337
   ISBN 0-9740015-0-3

   1. Florida--Officials and employees--Selections and appointment.   2. Florida--Politics and government--1951-
I. Title.

JK4458.M33 2003   352.6'5'097
                              QBI33-1301

Interior Design and Typesetting by Publishing Professionals, Port Richey, FL
Publishing Coordination by Sylvia Hemmerly
Cover Design by Sara L. Gardner
Photography by Ron Gardner Photography, Tallahassee, FL

The paper used in this publication meets the minimum requirements of the American National Standard for Information Sciences-Permanence of paper for printed library materials.

All rights reserved. No part of this publication may be reproduced, stored in a retrieval system, or transmitted, in any form or by any means, electronic, mechanical, photocopying, recording, or otherwise, without the expressed written consent of the author, with the exception of the public information.

*This book is dedicated to my daughters,
Sydney and Jennifer.
I hope that you are inspired to follow your dreams.
Without dreams, we will never reach our full potential
in life, so dream big, girls!
Have courage, faith and always, my love.*

Table of Contents

Preface vii
Acknowledgments ix
Introduction xi
How to Use this Book xiii

Tips, Advice, and Methods for
Gaining a Political Appointment

1   How to get a Political Appointment 3

Appointing Authorities and Phone Numbers

2   Florida Appointing Authorities 15

State Boards and Commissions

3   Agriculture / Environment / Wildlife /
    Water Resources 29
4   Arts / Entertainment / Tourism 45
5   Business / Economic Development /
    Workforce Innovation 55
6   Corrections / Courts / Juvenile Justice /
    Law Enforcement 75
7   Judicial Appointments 85
8   Education 91
9   Health / Health Care Administration /
    Elder Affairs 107
10 Social Services / Community Affairs /
    Veterans Affairs 139
11 Planning & Oversight / Federal, State &
    Regional Concerns / Military 153

12	Transportation / Highway Safety & Motor Vehicles / Public Utilities	167
13	Governor's Executive Office Staff	187
Appendix 1	Application form for Gubernatorial Appointment	191
Appendix 2	Application form for a Judicial Appointment	199
Index		213
About the Author		221

Preface

A Call For Citizen Leaders

Our Founding Fathers envisioned a country that would be governed by citizen leaders, people who would step forward to serve their country by contributing their time, talent, and passion in the service of our democracy. These citizen leaders would come from all cultural, ethnic and economic backgrounds, represent different geographic locations, and hold diverse opinions in order to ensure that the government best reflects the people it serves.

Though today many people are *elected* into government office, there are hundreds of positions in every state filled by citizen leaders who are appointed, and whose roles are equally important in government. They listen to the needs and concerns of our people, study problems, and propose solutions. Now more than ever, citizens are needed to uphold this vision of public service. There is great opportunity for men and women who want to lead their communities into a new century, far beyond the expectations of those who have served before.

So I call upon you, the legitimate heirs to the visions of our founders, to respond to the legacy of public service. Look inside yourself and find that true American spirit, because somewhere within your community or in the corridors of government there is an empty space for you to fill, an ideal for you to uphold, a message for you to send, and a hand for you to hold.

America is an unending sea of promise, possibility and privilege. Such abundant potential exists. Our cherished democracy, is not "free," but comes at a price; a mortgage of service, a repayment of action, a debt we owe to each other. I encourage you to take this opportunity to make your personal contribution by giving of yourself in one of the most important ways in which any American can—by stepping forward and becoming a citizen leader.

Acknowledgments

This book would not have been possible without the love and support of my husband Dennis. He has always encouraged me to pursue my goals and he has, by example, taught me to take risks, to be flexible, and to laugh. I am grateful everyday for his love.

Additionally, I would like to thank my editors, Willy Mathes and Kimberly Grunden, whose encouragement helped pull me across the finish line; and Sylvia Hemmerly at Publishing Professionals, for her guidance and support, as well as her dedicated team of designers, typesetters and marketing specialists.

The staff in Governor Jeb Bush's appointments' office was incredibly helpful; I am grateful for their aid and support, especially Ricardo Rodriguez and Mavis Knight. Thank you.

Some of the information contained in this book was developed from a review of the Constitution of the state of Florida, the Florida Statutes, the laws of Florida, and from county ordinances. Additional sources of information have come from the www.myflorida.com website and the Florida Bar website.

Also, I must acknowledge the brilliant women I worked with in California, especially the National Women's Political Caucus and the California Coalition for Women. They are all strong, opinionated, and funny ladies who have always inspired me. I treasure the lessons I learned from all of them.

And finally, Mom, for always being there with love and support. Thank you.

THE FLORIDA GUIDE TO POLITICAL APPOINTMENTS

Introduction

Can you imagine how great it would be to advise the mayor, the governor or even the president of the United States? Could you get excited about being in a position where you might influence the decisions these leaders make? It's not as far-fetched as you might think. Everyday, ordinary Americans are asked to provide guidance to our elected leaders by serving on advisory boards and commissions. Some even get paid for this service. So why is it that you haven't been asked? Perhaps it's simply because you haven't made your interest known . . . or maybe it's because you don't even *know* about the possibilities that are out there for you.

Since politicians have traditionally used these powerful government advisory appointments as a way to "repay" friends for their campaign support, it's no wonder that very little was known about the process. Now, however, times are changing. Every public administration needs the input of the community to make informed decisions and to ensure that they are representing the people that elected them. More attention is being paid to appointing a diverse mix of people; many legislatures, in fact, are mandating it. All of this adds up to an opportunity for you!

Why should you care about this often-overlooked opportunity? For one, in examining the resumes of politicians, top business leaders and other influential people, I have found a common qualification. Not the Ivy League education, a large bank account or even a well-connected relative. It is having received a political appointment at some point in their career. Many people use this form of public service as a stepping-stone to run for office and to hold leadership roles in business and community groups.

Adding an advisory board appointment or service on a commission to your resume is a boost in every sense of the word. It signifies that you are well informed, well connected and have real leadership potential. To illustrate the importance, imagine you're a nurse and the governor just appointed you to serve on the State Board of Nursing. Wouldn't your boss be impressed? You may even get that promotion you have been waiting for. Or, picture yourself as a restaurant owner and the mayor selects you to be on the local Tourism Development Council. Don't you think you would be able to use your knowledge and position on the board to help your business be more successful?

And finally, what if you were asked to serve on the city planning commission? You would soon figure out that the people who run our government are not really any smarter than you are; and that you, too, have the capacity to lead, and that you *are* qualified to run for office. Think about it: just serving on a board or commission gives you instant credibility.

Impeding you, of course, is the lack of a single source for information on available appointments, a guide to explain the mysterious nature of the whole process, and the mistaken assumption that you need to be an expert in some little known field to be qualified. That is why I have written this book. To provide the information you need to have a shot at obtaining a coveted appointment. This simple, easy-to-use "handbook" offers both the political novice and the savvy veteran clear insight into the state of Florida's appointment process, the positions that exist, and the kind of qualifications you may or may not need. Now that you're on the verge of being informed about political appointments, I say, "GO FOR IT!" After all, what do you have to lose?

How to Use this Book

For your convenience, all of the tips, advice, and methods for gaining a political appointment are up front in Chapter One. Including advice for senior level appointments in state government and what to do after you are appointed.

In Chapter Two you will find a current list of appointing authorities and phone numbers. Use these phone numbers to obtain up-to-date information on vacancies and request application forms. This chapter is especially important for individuals seeking local and regional appointments. Every city and county has different boards; so you must locate your city and/or county in the phone list, and then call the appointment coordinator directly for more information. In smaller cities, you may need to speak with the city or county administrator's office.

In Chapters 3-13 you will find some 400+ state boards and commissions listed by area of interest. These state level appointments are made primarily by the governor; therefore these chapters contain information on the boards, commissions, senior level and staff positions to which he or she makes the appointment. Once you have found the board or commission you are interested in—by reading through the descriptions and qualifications—use the phone list to contact the governor's appointments' office to request a vacancy list and an application form. Don't be concerned if the board or commission you are interested in doesn't have a vacancy at the time you call—because vacancies occur on a regular basis—and you will need some time to prepare. Because the Speaker of the House and the president of the state senate also make appointments to many of the same governor-appointed boards, you may want to contact them as well. State constitutional officers, cabinet secretaries, and department heads have some appointing authority and may create their own advisory boards. The more you investigate your options, the more opportunities you will find.

Keep in mind that the process is the same at every level of appointment you seek. The only difference is the competition and the type of "campaign" you will need to be successful. I am writing this book because, when I first heard about political appointments and considered whether or not I could obtain one, I felt scared and intimidated. I became convinced it was nearly impossible for "someone like me" to be appointed. But my experience quickly showed me that such assumptions are flat-out wrong! I have found that this is actually one of the easiest ways for people to take an active role in government. I urge you to pursue an appointment as a way of making a difference and as a way to gain experience for greater involvement in the future.

If not now, then when? If not you, then who?

Tips, Advice, and Methods for
Gaining a Political Appointment

How to get a political appointment in the state of Florida

The aim of this book is to give you the information needed to obtain a political appointment in Florida. The words "political appointment" make it clear that this is a highly political process. Understanding just what that means is vital to your success. It is not an accidental event if you are selected to serve as an advisor to your local mayor or the governor, and since it is highly unlikely that you will be selected out of obscurity to serve, this book offers experience-based guidance and advice that can be useful at every appointed level. Whether you want to become a senior staffer to the governor or you just want to solve a problem in your own community by serving locally, there are a few things you should keep in mind.

1. **Timing is important.** When a new mayor takes office, he or she will have to make anywhere from a few dozen to several hundred appointments; a new governor will literally make thousands of appointments in his or her first term in office. By identifying what position(s) you're interested in by thoroughly reviewing the descriptions and qualifications in Chapters 3–13, and by finding out when vacancies for those positions will occur, you can plan your "action steps" most effectively.

2. **Being seen in the right places is helpful.** This will allow you to develop key contacts and gain name recognition as one of the appointer's key supporters.
3. **You should be somewhat qualified for the position you are seeking.** Being the "most qualified" person for the position isn't as important as you may think. However, you should be able to demonstrate a good understanding of the issues.
4. **The ability to garner the support of the right people is essential.** Gaining an appointment requires the support of people or organizations whom the appointer trusts. At some point, "insiders" (and "outsiders," too, for that matter) will weigh in on your potential appointment; unless you truly are one of those "insiders" to begin with, then getting recommendations from people close to the appointer is critical.
5. **Most importantly you have to apply.** After you have done all of the "footwork" (see below), apply in written form by filling out an application. Remember, dropping hints in verbal conversations with the appointer simply won't do. Make your aspirations clear in writing and then go for it, *but read on to make sure you know how to run an effective campaign.*

First Things First:

Decide why you want an appointment. Are you doing it to enhance your career? Do you want an appointment to add to your resume for a future run for office? Or, are you simply a concerned citizen that has a particular interest and wants to be on the front line of solving problems? Your reasons for applying will help to direct you towards the most appropriate position(s). For example, if you are trying to enhance your career with an appointment, you may apply for something related to your chosen profession. Getting an appointment will impress your boss, give you more credibility in your field, and enhance your existing business knowledge. If you want to run for office someday, then you may try to get appointed to a board that deals with issues which will add to your knowledge base and give you a broader platform from which to campaign. If you are seeking an appointment to make a contribution to your community, then choose a commission that studies the problem you want to solve.

Once you have an understanding of your objective in seeking an appointment, it will be easier to target a board or commission that meets your needs. Be flexible and patient; you may have to wait for a vacancy to occur.

When an opportunity does open up, be certain of who is the appointing authority to fill that particular vacancy, as many boards and commissions get their appointees from different sources. For example, most transportation boards are comprised of appointments made by the governor, county commissioners, and perhaps from the mayor's office or the city council. Another example is a commission made up of people selected by the governor, the Speaker of the House, and a state constitutional officer, such as the attorney general. So again, be sure you know who the appointing authority is for the position you are seeking before you begin your campaign. Also, keep in mind that the announced vacancy may not be a vacancy at all, just an expired term of service for which the incumbent board member will likely be reappointed. This often happens, especially if there is no serious opposition to his or her reappointment, no real reason to make a change, or if no one else applies. However, *if* someone else applies, runs a strong campaign, and has something interesting to contribute that appeals to the appointer, who knows what might happen?

Tips and Words of Advice:

While researching appointments in Florida, I found that there is no single source of information on the subject. The state website is incomplete, often out-of-date, and simply doesn't provide the kind of inside information that will get you an appointment. So, the following is my advice based on years of studying appointment behavior and helping people through the process.

Here is what you need to do:

- **Find a way to attain some positive name recognition.** You want the appointer and the people who surround him or her to remember your name when they see it on the list of possible candidates for appointment. You can achieve this in a number of different ways; some examples might include starting a scholarship or community event or receiving publicity for your business success.

- **Show up at events.** Speeches, meetings and other events attended by the candidate/appointer are great opportunities to make contact. This is never the right time to lobby for an appointment; just focus on making a good impression.

- **Attend political fund-raising events.** Giving money signals that you are interested and invested in the candidate's success. The amount given is not as important as giving it. Often, a small amount is enough to get recognized and placed in the appointer's database of "friends." Raising money by hosting an event yourself, or by selling tickets for a campaign-sponsored fund-raiser will put you in an even better category—that of "major supporter."

- **Make friends with the appointer's campaign advisors or paid political consultants.** Let these people know you are a supporter and that you can be helpful in delivering a certain group of voters, or that you are willing to help organize a fund-raiser. Organize a neighborhood rally or a breakfast with important people in your neighborhood, and then coordinate with campaign advisors to get the candidate to attend. This serves two purposes: it will get you recognized, and it will increase your value to the appointer.

- **Check campaign contribution reports.** The campaign's largest donors are just the kind of influential people and organizations you want to get to know. Make sure they know your name and who you are; it is helpful to have a friend or acquaintance who can pick up the phone and get through to the appointer.

- **Bring something to the table, votes being the most appreciated.** Do you have a certain natural constituency? Do you belong to a large voting block? Are you in a position to influence that block? If not, work on it. Become the head of your union, chamber of commerce, or women's organization and make sure the appointing authority knows it. Votes are more valuable than money. So, if you are in a position to rally support, then use that to your full advantage.

- **Remain flexible.** Be open-minded and flexible throughout this process and apply for more than one position. I recommend that you use separate application forms for each board or commission. There is no way to be sure of manual filing systems or the way in which your application may be filed, so cover all of the bases by using separate forms for each position. Also, do a thorough follow-up to ensure the application is received by the appropriate person.

- **Cultivate "friends in high places."** Knowing influential people who can write letters of support for you is important. This group should include politicians, business leaders, non-profit and community leaders, political donors, advisors, and anyone else who has influence with the appointer. Before asking for letters of recommendation, be sure that they themselves are in good standing with the appointer. You don't want a recommendation from someone who is at odds with the appointer, no matter how "important" the person is making the recommendation. Recommendations from people who are completely unknown to the appointer are also of little value. If you do not have well-placed supporters to write for you, then start by associating yourself with groups that will lead to that. It is surprisingly easy to get a meeting with a politician, especially if you happen to be their constituent. Taking the time to investigate your choice of references and only selecting well-placed people *will* pay off. I guarantee it.

- **Provide a sample letter for your reference to use as a guide.** Often, a person whom you have asked to send a letter of recommendation appreciates receiving a sample letter. This lets them know specifically what their letter should include. Don't assume that they need a sample letter. Rather, ask if this would be helpful to them, and then send it promptly. In fact, you should have this letter ready to go even before you ask. It is also a good idea to send a thank-you letter to let them know how much you appreciate their help, and that you may wish to call on them again.

- **Marketing is very important.** Once you have donated, been to the parties, lined up supporters, and found a group of voters to represent, then put together a package highlighting these things. Don't just send in an application form; send a folder with a resume, a short narrative biography of your life, work, accomplishments, and other important information that doesn't necessarily appear on your resume or in the application. Include copies of any letters of recommendation you receive, as well as press clippings about yourself or your work. As much as possible, tailor your materials to the position, and, of course, make sure that you have someone proofread everything thoroughly. The information you supply should be in an easy-to-photocopy format, as it may need to be reproduced for several board members or for a meeting.

- **Monitor the process.** Know when the decision will be made. Time letters of recommendation and phone calls from your supporters to coincide with the decision-making process. That way, you and the potential support you offer will not be forgotten by the appointer when it comes time to make a choice.

- **Send thank-you notes.** Everyone who helped you should receive one, including those who interviewed you. Remember, you may need them in the future. Take the opportunity to re-emphasize your strengths in the thank you note.

- **Don't give up.** Once the decision has been made, if you are not selected for appointment, my emphatic advice is, "Don't give up!" Many times, appointments are made for reasons unknown, and frankly, unknowable to you. That doesn't mean you are not a good candidate for an appointment or that a future campaign won't successfully garner you the appointment you seek. Call the appointer's staff and let them know that you really want to serve. Ask for their help in finding the appropriate board or commission for you. You are on the right track, and something will eventually fit.

Senior level appointments and key staff positions:

- **Be well connected.** People who have worked closely with the appointing authority or have a personal or professional relationship with them, are, of course, most likely to be considered for appointment. However, people who have contributed to the appointer's campaign in a noteworthy way, people who have a significant record of accomplishment, and especially people who can deliver a constituency of voters, are also in a good position to receive a high level appointment.

- **Get professional help.** If you are attempting to gain a high level appointment, you may want to consider using a political consultant yourself. A consultant will help you with the details and can put you on the right path by getting you invited to the best events. A consultant will help package your application materials and market you for the position. Professional advice is always a plus. If you do seek professional advice for your campaign, begin early; and whenever possible, use the same consulting firm the appointer uses. Contact the firm well before election day to explain your interests and qualifications for appointment, and as mentioned in the tips section, express your willingness to help the candidate/appointer.

- **Marketing is critical.** If you can't afford professional help, then make sure your application package and everything in it is flawless and presented in a professional manner. Your chances improve significantly if you present yourself with the same or better "quality consciousness" as everyone else vying for the appointment.

- **Be an active agent on your own behalf.** You must, at least initially, wage your own campaign. After you have completed the first few steps, however, back off and allow your supporters to work for you. You should still control the tone and message of their efforts, but stay behind the scenes; this is when all of your pre-election work pays off.

- **Find a balance.** It is sometimes difficult to make a distinction between self-promotion and the "honor of" just being considered. Too much politicking can backfire, so be as tactful as possible in your campaign.

- **See the "big picture."** Some considerations the appointer makes when selecting appointees include: the wishes of people he or she may owe a political debt to, the feelings and agenda of powerful special interest groups, and whether or not the appointee will grant special interest groups the support of his or her constituency of voters. The appointer is mindful of his or her own political agenda and your ability to help implement or articulate that same vision.

- **Stay out of the media.** The less the public and media know about your campaign to be appointed, the less opposition you will face, so do not actively seek media attention or public support. Special interest groups who are friendly to the appointer, especially those acting at the highest level and with a great amount of confidentiality, are useful to involve. Be aware that if opposition interest groups become involved the media will pick it up, which usually has a negative impact on your chance of being appointed.

- **Work on the campaign.** If you are seeking a staff position, this is usually done by working on the candidate's campaign. It is a gamble, but you must target your candidate well before election day and work hard to make sure that he or she is elected. This doesn't necessarily mean you need to quit your job and go to work on the campaign; you can work for the campaign by organizing events and/or fund-raisers, making or soliciting donations, and doing everything possible to be perceived as a valuable member of the campaign team. Quietly make it known that you would like to be involved in the new administration in whatever capacity you can be of most use. Don't pick a position for yourself, as this is usually a mistake. Instead, pick an area you would like to work in, such as the press, scheduling, or legislative fields. Then, during the campaign, align yourself with the insiders, family, business partners, and people who will be in the candidate's life, no matter what happens. Don't be too pushy or too friendly, and always be professional. Consider this a very long interview for the job you really want.

When you finally get an appointment, there are a few things you should do to get off to the right start.

- **Send thank you notes.** Thank everyone who helped you along the way. This often-overlooked act is "money in the bank" for future endeavors, and the people who helped you will remember your gesture.

- **Set up an informational meeting.** Schedule a time to meet with the board, commission chair or with key staff members to be briefed on any major issues you will face. Take this opportunity to review the upcoming agenda, so that you will feel confident going into your first hearing.

- **Set up a meeting with the appointer.** Schedule a meeting with their legislative staff, so that you can be sure you know the appointer's position on key issues. At this time, you may receive direction on upcoming votes and also find out other important information that will help you to be more effective.

- **Take this time to listen carefully.** You already have the job, now learn from people who have been there or helped you to get there. Don't be too quick to form opinions. Try not to voice any of your existing opinions, either . . . at least until you have all the facts, and especially not before you receive direction from the appointer. There may be larger implications for positions than are initially apparent to you.

- **Congratulations!** You are on your way to positively influencing your government and community. Remember, in politics, as in life, one thing always leads to another, and this is just the beginning. So, with a clear and heartfelt intention to both serve and lead others in your community, and with a willingness to do what it takes to meet the needs of each arising situation, step forward now into the open field of possibilities before you and *make a difference!*

Appointing Authorities and Phone Numbers

Florida Appointing Authorities

The following appointing authorities make appointments to a wide variety of boards, commissions, councils and advisory groups, as well as to senior level and staff positions. The appointments that these authorities make, both as individuals and as a group, range from gubernatorial appointments of the highest power, such as supreme court justice or secretary of state, to appointments made by the collective members of your city council, to advisory boards that deal with many community needs, including local housing, transportation or health care. Many of these appointments, even at the local level, can have regional and statewide significance, so don't assume that only appointments made by the governor are important. Contact each appointing authority's office directly to obtain a complete list of the bodies for which they make appointments, an application form, and an up-to-date list of vacancies. The following phone lists will aid you with your inquires. Another good source of information is the myflorida.com website.

State Appointments

Statewide office holders:

Governor
850-488-4441

Attorney General
850-487-1963

State Chief Executive Office
850-413-3100

Commissioner of Agriculture
850-488-3022

The President of the State Senate of Florida
850-487-5229

The Speaker of the House for the State of Florida
850-488-1450

Local and Regional Appointments:
Contact the county and the city in which you live.

County Commission Offices
See county listing

City Mayors Office
See city listing

City Council Offices
See city listing

Phone List of Cities by County

Alachua County
(352) 374-5210

Alachua
(386) 462-1231

Archer
(352) 495-2880

Gainsville
(352) 334-5005

Hawthorne
(352) 481-2432

High Springs
(904) 454-1416

La Crosse
(352) 462-2784

Micanopy
(352) 466-3121

Newberry
(352) 472-2161

Waldo
(352) 468-1001

Baker County
(904) 259-2403

Glen Saint Mary
(904) 259-3777

Macclenny
(904) 259-6261

Bay County
(850) 784-4013

Callaway
(850) 871-6000

Cedar Grove
(850) 763-2911

Lynn Haven
(850) 265-2121

Mexico Beach
(850) 648-5700

Panama City
(850) 872-3000

Panama City Beach
(850) 233-5100

Parker
(850) 871-4104

Springfield
(850) 872-7570

Bradford County
(904) 964-6250

Brooker
(352) 485-1022

Hampton
(352) 468-1201

Lawtey
(804) 782-3454

Starke
(904) 964-5027

Brevard County
(321) 633-2000

Cape Canaveral
(321) 868-1230

Cocoa
(321) 639-7555

Cocoa Beach
(321) 868-3333

Indialantic
(321) 723-2242

Indian Harbour Beach
(321) 773-3181

Malabar
(321) 727-7764

Melbourne
(321) 727-2900

Melbourne Beach
(321) 724-5680

Melbourne Village
(321) 723-8300

Palm Bay
(321) 952-3400

Palm Shores
(321) 242-4555

Rockledge
(321) 690-3978

Satellite Beach
(321) 773-4407

Titusville
(321) 383-5775

West Melbourne
(321) 727-7700

Broward County
(954) 357-7354

Coconut Creek
(954) 973-6770

Cooper City
(954) 434-4300

Coral Springs
(954) 344-1000

Dania Beach
(954) 924-3600

Davie
(954) 797-1000

Deerfield Beach
(954) 480-4200

Fort Lauderdale
(954) 828-5000

Hallandale Beach
(954) 457-1300

THE FLORIDA GUIDE TO POLITICAL APPOINTMENTS

Hillsboro Beach
(954) 427-4011

Hollywood
(954) 921-3211

Lauderdale Lakes
(954) 535-2700

Lauderdale-by-the-Sea
(954) 776-0576

Lauderhill
(954) 739-0100

Lazy Lake
(954) 565-1567

Lightbouse Point
(954) 943-6500

Margate
(954) 972-6454

Miramar
(954) 967-1500

North Lauderdale
(954) 722-0900

Oakland Park
(954) 561-6250

Parkland
(954) 753-5040

Pembroke Park
(954) 966-4600

Pembroke Pines
(954) 431-4500

Plantation
(954) 797-2200

Pompano Beach
(954) 786-4600

Sea Ranch Lakes
(954) 943-8862

Southwest Ranches
(954) 434-0008

Sunrise
(954) 741-2580

Tamarac
(954) 385-2000

Wilton Manors
(954) 390-2100

Calhoun County
850-674-6215

Altha
(850) 762-3280

Blounstown
(850) 674-5488

Charlotte County
(941) 743-1300

Punta Gorda
(941) 575-3369

Citrus County
(352) 341-6560

Crystal River
(352) 795-4216

Inverness
(352) 726-2611

Clay County
(904) 284-6335

Green Cove Springs
(904) 529-2200

Keystone Heights
(352) 473-4807

Orange Park
(904) 278-3018

Penney Farms
(904) 529-9078

Collier County
(239) 774-8097

Everglades City
(941) 695-3781

Marco Island
(941) 389-5000

Naples
(941) 213-1030

Columbia County
(386) 758-1005

Fort White
(386) 497-2321

Lake City
(386) 752-2031

DeSoto County
(863) 993-4800

Arcadia
(863) 494-4114

Dixie County
(352) 498-1206

Cross City
(352) 498-3306

HorshoeBeach
(352) 498-5234

Duval County
(904) 630-1377

Atlantic Beach
(904) 247-5800

Baldwin
(904) 266-4221

Jacksonville
(904) 630-1178

Jacksonville Beach
(904) 247-6268

Neptune Beach
(904) 270-2400

Escambia County
(850) 595-4902

Century
(850) 256-3208

18

Pensacola
(850) 435-1603

Flagler County
(386) 437-7480

    Beverly Beach
    (386) 439-6888

    Bunnell
    (386) 437-7500

    Flagler Beach
    (386) 517-2000

    Marineland
    (904) 461-4044

    Palm Coast
    (386) 447-4255

Franklin County
(850) 653-8861

    Apalachicola
    (850) 653-9319

    Carrabelle
    (850) 697-3618

Gadsden County
(800) 875-8650

    Chattahoochee
    (850) 663-4046

    Greensboro
    (850) 442-6215

    Gretna
    (850) 856-5257

    Havana
    (850) 539-6493

    Midway
    (850) 574-2355

    Quincy
    (850) 627-7681

Gilchrist County
(352) 463-3170

    Bell
    (352) 463-6288

    Fanning Springs
    (352) 463-2855

    Trenton
    (352) 463-4000

Glades County
(863) 946-6002

    Moore Haven
    (863) 946-0711

Gulf County
(850) 229-6106

    Port St. Joe
    (850) 229-8261

    Wewahitchka
    (850) 639-2606

Hamilton County
(386) 792-6639

    Jasper
    (386) 792-1212

    Jennings
    (386) 938-4131

    White Springs
    (386) 397-2310

Hardee County
(863) 773-6952

    Bowling Green
    (863) 375-2255

    Wauchula
    (863) 773-3131

    ZolfoSprings
    (863) 735-0405

Hendry County
(863) 675-5216

    Clewiston
    (863) 983-1484

    Labelle
    (863) 675-2872

Hernando County
(352) 544-5400

    Weeki Wachee
    (352) 592-2004

Highlands County
(863) 402-6500

    Avon Park
    (863) 452-4400

    Lake Placid
    (863) 699-3747

    Sebring
    (863) 471-5100

Hillsborough County
(813) 272-5660

    Plant City
    (813) 659-4200

    Tampa
    (813) 274-8211

    Temple Terrace
    (813) 989-7100

Holmes County
(850) 547-1119

    Bonifay
    (850) 547-4238

    Esto
    (850) 263-6521

    Noma
    (850) 263-3449

Ponce De Leon
(850) 836-4361

Westville
(850) 548-5858

Indian River County
(772) 567-8000

Fellsmere
(772) 571-1616

Indian River Shores
(561) 231-1771

Orchid
(561) 589-6100

Sebastian
(561) 589-5330

Vero Beach
(772) 978-5151

Jackson County
(850) 482-9633

Alford
(850) 579-4684

Bascom
(850) 569-2634

Campbelton
(850) 263-4535

Cottondale
(850) 352-4361

Graceville
(850) 263-3250

Grand Ridge
(850) 592-4621

Greenwood
(850) 594-1216

Jacob City
(850) 263-6636

Malone
(850) 569-2308

Marianna
(850) 482-4353

Sneada
(850) 593-6636

Jefferson County
(850) 997-2036

Monticello
(850) 342-0153

Lafayette County
(386) 294-1325

Mayo
(386) 294-1551

Lake County
(352) 342-9850

Astula
(352) 742-1100

Clermont
(352) 394-4081

Eustis
(352) 483-5430

Fruitland Park
(352) 787-6089

Groveland
(352) 429-2141

Howey-in-the-Hills
(352) 324-2290

Lady Lake
(352) 751-1500

Leesburg
(352) 728-9700

Mascotte
(352) 429-3341

Minneola
(352) 394-3598

Montverde
(407) 469-2681

Mount Dora
(352) 735-7100

Tavares
(352) 742-6209

Umatilla
(352) 669-3125

Lee County
(239) 335-2259

Bonita Springs
(941) 390-1000

Cape Coral
(941) 574-0401

Fort Myers
(941) 332-6700

Fort Myers Beach
(941) 765-0202

Sanibel
(941) 472-4135

Leon County
(850) 488-4710

Tallahassee
(850) 891-0010

Levy County
(352) 486-5217

Bronson
(352) 486-2354

Cedar Key
(352) 543-5132

Chiefland
(352) 493-6711

Fanning Springs
(352) 463-2855

Inglis
(352) 447-2203

Otter Creek
(352) 486-4413

Williston
(352) 528-3060

Yankeetown
(352) 447-2511

Liberty County
(850) 643-2215

Bristol
(850) 643-2261

Madison County
(850) 973-3179

Greenville
(850) 948-2251

Lee
(850) 971-5867

Madison
(850) 973-5081

Manatee County
(941) 745-3700

Anna Maria
(941) 708-6130

Bradenton
(941) 708-6800

Brandenton Beach
(941) 778-1005

Holmes Beach
(941) 708-5800

Palmetto
(941) 723-4570

Longboat Key
(941) 316-1999

Marion County
(352) 620-3307

Belleview
(352) 245-7021

Dunnellon
(352) 489-2423

McIntosh
(352) 591-1047

Ocala
(352) 629-8401

Reddick
(352) 591-1332

Martin County
(772) 288-5420

Jupiter Island
(561) 546-5011

Ocean Breeze Park
(772) 334-2494

Sewall's Point
(772) 287-2455

Stuart
(561) 288-5312

Miami-Dade County
(305) 375-5124

Aventura
(305) 466-8900

Bal Harbour
(305) 866-4633

Bay Harbor Islands
(305) 866-6241

Biscayne Park
(305) 893-7490

Coral Gables
(305) 446-6800

El Portal
(305) 795-7880

Florida City
(305) 247-8221

Golden Beach
(305) 932-0744

Hialeah
(305) 883-5800

Hialeah Gardens
(305) 558-4114

Homestead
(305) 247-1801

Indian Creek
(305) 865-4121

Islandia
none available

Key Biscayne
(305) 365-5511

Medley
(305) 887-9541

Miami
(305) 250-5300

Miami Beach
(305) 673-7000

Miami Lakes
(305) 558-8244

Miami Shores Village
(305) 795-2207

Miami Springs
(305) 805-5000

North Bay Village
(305) 756-7171

North Miami
(305) 893-6511

North Miami Beach
(305) 947-7581

Opa-Locka
(305) 688-4611

Pinecrest
(305) 234-2121

South Miami
(305) 663-6338

Sunny Isles Beach
(305) 947-0606

Surfside
(305) 861-4863

Sweetwater
(305) 221-0411

Virginia Gardens
(305) 871-6104

West Miami
(305) 266-1122

Monroe County
(305) 292-4441

Islamorda
(305) 664-2345

Key Colony Beach
(305) 289-1212

Key West
(305) 292-8200

Layton
(305) 664-4667

Marathon
(305) 743-0033

Nassau County
(704) 321-5703

Callahan
(904) 879-3801

Fernandina Beach
(904) 277-7305

Hilliard
(904) 845-3555

Okaloosa County
(850) 589-5030

Cinco Bayou
(850) 833-3406

Crestview
(850) 682-1091

Destin
(850) 837-4242

Fort Walton Beach
(850) 833-9509

Laurel Hill
(850) 652-4441

Mary Esther
(850) 243-3566

Niceville
(850) 729-4000

Shalimar
(850) 651-5723

Valparaiso
(850) 729-5402

Okachobee County
(863) 763-6441

Okachobee
(863) 763-3372

Orange County
(407) 836-7350

Apopka
(407) 703-1700

Bay Lake
(407) 826-2241

Belle Isle
(407) 851-7730

Eatonville
(407) 623-1313

Edgewood
(407) 851-2920

Lake Buena Vista
(407) 826-2241

Maitland
(407) 539-6200

Oakland
(407) 656-1117

Ocoee
(407) 905-3100

Orlando
(407) 246-2121

Windermere
(407) 876-2563

Winter Garden
(407) 656-4111

Winter Park
(407) 599-3399

Osceola County
(407) 343-2200

Kissimmee
(407) 847-2821

St. Cloud
(407) 957-7301

Palm Beach County
(561) 996-4815

Atlantis
(561) 965-1744

Belle Glade
(561) 996-0100

Boca Raton
(561) 393-7700

Boynton Beach
(561) 742-6000

Briny Breezes
(561) 276-7406

Cloud Lake
(561) 686-2815

Delray Beach
(561) 243-7000

Glen Ridge
(561) 697-8686

Golf
(561) 732-0236

Greenacres
(561) 642-2006

Gulf Stream
(561) 276-5116

Haverhill
(561) 689-0370

Highland Beach
(561)278-4546

Hypoluxo
(561) 582-0155

Juno Beach
(561) 626-1122

Jupiter
(561) 746-5134

Jupiter Inlet Colony
(561) 746-3787

Lake Clarke Shores
(561) 964-1515

Lake Park
(561) 881-3300

Lake Worth
(561) 586-1600

Lantana
(561) 540-5000

Manalapan
(561) 585-9477

Mangonia Park
(561) 848-1235

North Palm Beach
(561) 841-3355

Ocean Ridge
(561) 732-2635

Pahokee
(561) 924-5534

Palm Beach
(561) 838-5410

Palm Beach Gardens
(561) 799-4100

Palm Beach Shores
(561) 844-3457

Palm Springs
(561) 965-4010

Rivera Beach
(561) 845-4000

Royal Palm Beach
(561) 790-5100

South Bay
(561) 996-6751

South Palm Beach
(561) 588-8889

Tequesta
(561) 578-6200

Wellington
(561) 791-4000

West Palm Beach
(561) 659-8000

Pasco County
(352) 521-4111

Dade City
(352) 523-5050

New Port Richey
(727) 841-4500

Port Richey
(727) 816-1900

San Antonio
(352) 588-2127

St. Leo
(352) 588-2622

Zephyrhills
(813) 780-0000

Pinellas County
(727) 464-3377

Belleair
(727) 588-3769

Belleair Beach
(727) 595-4646

Belleair Bluffs
(727) 584-2151

Belleair Shore
(727) 593-9296

Clearwater
(727) 562-4040

Dunedin
(727) 298-3000

Gulfport
(727) 893-1000

Indian Rocks Beach
(727) 595-2517

Indian Shores
(727) 595-4020

Pinellas County
(727) 464-3485

Kenneth City
(727) 544-6655

Largo
(727) 587-6700

Madeira Beach
(727) 391-9591

North Redington Beach
(727) 391-4848

Oldsmar
(813) 855-4693

Pinellas Park
(727) 541-0700

Redington Beach
(727) 391-3875

Redington Shores
(727) 397-5538

Safety Harbor
(727) 724-1555

Seminole
(727) 391-0204

South Pasadena
(727) 347-4171

St. Pete Beach
(727) 367-2738

St. Petersburg
(727) 893-7201

Tarpon Springs
(727) 938-3711

Treasure Island
(727) 547-4575

Polk County
(863) 534-6000

Auburndale
(863) 965-5500

Bartow
(863) 534-0100

Davenport
(863) 419-3300

Dundee
(863) 419-3100

Eagle Lake
(863) 293-4141

Fort Meade
(863) 285-1100

Frostproof
(863) 635-7855

Haines City
(863) 421-3600

Highland Park
(863) 676-6325

Hillcrest Heights
(863) 638-2732

Lake Alfred
(863) 291-5270

Lake Hamilton
(863) 439-1910

Lake Wales
(863) 678-4182

Lakeland
(863) 834-6000

Mulberry
(863) 425-1125

Polk City
(863) 984-1375

Winter Haven
(863) 291-5611

Putnam County
(386) 329-0200

Crescent City
(904) 698-2525

Interlachen
(386) 684-3811

Palatka
(386) 329-0100

Pomona Park
(386) 649-4902

Welaka
(386) 467-9800

Santa Rosa County
(850) 983-1002

Gulf Breeze
(850) 934-5100

Jay
(850) 675-4556

Milton
(850) 983-5410

Sarasota County
(941) 951-5111

Longboat Key
(941) 316-1999

North Port
(941) 426-8484

Sarasota
(941) 365-2200

Venice
(941) 486-2626

Seminole County
(407) 655-7219

Altamonte Springs
(407) 571-8000

Casselberry
(407) 262-7700

Lake Mary
(407) 585-1400

Longwood
(407) 260-3440

Oviedo
(407) 977-6000

Sanford
(407) 330-5600

Winter Springs
(407) 327-1800

St. Johns County
(904) 823-2400

Hastings
(904) 662-1420

Marinefield
(904) 461-4044

St. Augustine
(904) 825-1005

St. Augustine Beach
(904) 471-2122

St. Lucie County
(772) 462-1400

Fort Pierce
(772) 460-2200

Port St. Lucie
(772) 871-5225

St. Lucie Village
(561) 466-6900

Sumter County
(352) 793-0200

Bushnell
(352) 793-2591

Center Hill
(352) 793-4431

Coleman
(352) 748-1017

Webster
(352) 793-2073

Wildwood
(352) 330-1330

Suwanee County
(386) 364-3450

    Branford
    (386) 935-1146

    Live Oak
    (386) 362-2276

Taylor County
(850) 835-3506

    Perry
    (850) 584-7161

Union County
(386) 496-4241

    Lake Butler
    (904) 496-3401

    Railford
    (904) 431-1955

    Worthington Springs
    (904) 496-1006

Volusia County
(386) 736-5920

    Daytona Beach
    (386) 671-8000

Daytona Beach Shore
(386) 322-5000

DeBary
(386) 668-2040

DeLand
(386) 740-5700

Deltona
(386) 561-2100

Edgewater
(386) 424-2400

Holly Hill
(386) 248-9441

Lake Helen
(386) 424-2121

New Smyrna Beach
(386) 424-2100

Oak Hill
(386) 345-3522

Orange City
(386) 775-5400

Ormond Beach
(386) 677-0311

Pierson
(904) 749-2661

Ponce Inlet
(386) 322-6711

Port Orange
(386) 756-5200

South Daytona
(386) 322-3010

Wakulla County
(850) 926-0919

    Sopchoppy
    (850) 962-4611

    St. Marks
    (850) 9258-6224

Walton County
(850) 892-8115

    DeFuniak Springs
    (850) 892-8500

    Freeport
    (850) 835-2822

    Paxton
    (850) 834-2716

Washington County
(850) 638-6200

    Caryville
    (850) 548-5571

    Chipley
    (850) 638-6350

    Ebro
    (850) 535-2842

    Vernon
    (850) 535-2444

    Wausau
    (850) 638-1781

State Boards and Commissions

Agriculture / Environment / Wildlife / Water Resources

The boards, commissions and senior level appointments listed in this chapter work with issues that safeguard the public and support Florida's agricultural economy, environment, wildlife, and water resources. They ensure the safety and wholesomeness of food and other consumer products, as well as regulate Florida's citrus industry. They protect, conserve, and manage Florida's environment through the management and regulation of water, water facilities, wetlands, beaches, air resources, solid and hazardous waste cleanup, marine resources, the mining, oil, and gas resources, state park systems, and state-owned land. Additionally, Florida's 5 regional water management districts preserve and conserve the state's water by monitoring water pollution, regulating the drawing of water from underground sources, and purchasing environmentally sensitive land to be included in the public domain.

In addition to the appointments mentioned in this chapter, the governor may fill vacancies due to resignation, death, removal, promotion, or other special circumstances. This includes appointments to elected bodies such as local water control, environmental control, and inlet management districts.

Senior Level Appointments:

Secretary of the Department of Environmental Protection

Executive Director of the Department of Citrus

Executive Director of the Fish and Wildlife Conservation Commission

Boards and Commissions:

Acquisition and Restoration Council

Authority: Section 259.035, Florida Statutes
Term: 4 years
Confirmation Required: None
Oversight: Department of Environmental Protection
Compensation: $75.00 per day of service + per diem, in accordance with Section 112.061 of the Florida Statutes
Description: The council shall provide assistance to the board of trustees of the Internal Improvement Trust Fund, in reviewing the recommendations and plans for the state-owned lands. The council shall, in reviewing such recommendation and plans, consider the optimization of multiple-use and conservation strategies to accomplish the provisions funded pursuant to Section 259.101(3)(a) of the Florida Statutes.
Qualifications: The council shall consist of 9 voting members, 4 appointed by the governor. The governor shall appoint the chair. No appointee shall serve more than 6 years. Members shall be from scientific disciplines related to land, water or environmental sciences.

Alligator Point Water Resources Board

Authority: Chapter 85-414, Laws of Florida
Term: 4 years
Confirmation Required: None
Oversight: County Jurisdiction

Compensation: Per diem, in accordance with Section 112.061 of the Florida Statutes
Description: The Water Resources Board of Alligator Point will construct and maintain a water system to provide fresh water in the district, and they will fix and collect rates charged for furnishing such water.
Qualifications: Members shall be property owners in the district. Members shall be appointed by the governor.

Apalachicola–Chattahoochee–Flint River Basin Commission

Authority: Section 373.71, Florida Statutes
Term: Pleasure of the Governor
Confirmation Required: None
Oversight: Federal Organization Titles
Compensation: Per diem, in accordance with Section 112.061 of the Florida Statutes
Description: The ACF River Basin Compact is a compact that the states of Alabama, Florida, and Georgia have with the United States government, which has been entered into for the purposes of promoting interstate comity, removing causes of present and future controversies, equitably apportioning the surface waters of the ACF, engaging in water planning, and developing and sharing common data bases.
Qualifications: The governor of each of the states shall serve as state commissioner. The governor shall appoint one or more alternate members. One alternate member may serve as state commissioner for the governor. Alternate members shall be knowledgeable about water resources management.

Atlantic States Marine Fisheries Commission

Authority: Section 370.19(2)
Term: 3 years
Confirmation Required: Senate
Oversight: Federal Organization Titles

Compensation: Per diem, in accordance with Section 112.061 of the Florida Statutes
Description: The commission ascertains such methods, practices, and conditions as may be disclosed for bringing about the conservation and prevention of the depletion and waste of Atlantic Seaboard fisheries.
Qualifications: The citizen member shall be appointed by the governor and shall have a knowledge of and an interest in the marine fisheries.

Boating Advisory Council

Authority: Section 327.803, Florida Statutes
Term: 2 years
Confirmation Required: None
Oversight: Fish and Wildlife Conservation Commission
Compensation: Per diem, in accordance with Section 112.061 of the Florida Statutes
Description: The purpose of the council is to make recommendations to the Fish and Wildlife Conservation Commission and the Department of Community Affairs regarding issues affecting the boating community: this includes boating and diving safety education; boating-related facilities, including marinas and boat testing facilities, and boat usage.
Qualifications: The council shall consist of 17 members, 10 appointed by the governor each of whom shall be nominated by the executive director of the Fish and Wildlife Conservation Commission.

Environmental Regulation Commission

Authority: Section 20.255(7) Florida Statutes
Term: 4 years
Confirmation Required: Senate
Oversight: Department of Environmental Protection
Compensation: Per diem, in accordance with Section 112.061 of the Florida Statutes

Description: The commission exercises the exclusive standard-setting authority of the Department of Environmental Regulation and has final state approval on grant application for the construction of water treatment works.
Qualifications: The commission shall be composed of 7 members appointed by the governor and confirmed by the senate. The governor shall appoint the chair. The governor shall provide reasonable representation from all sections of the state.

Fish and Wildlife Conservation Commission

Authority: Article IV, Section 9, Florida Constitution
Term: 5 years
Confirmation Required: Senate
Oversight: Fish and Wildlife Conservation Commission
Compensation: Per diem, in accordance with Section 112.061 of the Florida Statutes
Description: The commission exercises the regulatory and executive powers of the state with respect to wild animal life and fresh water aquatic life. They also exercise regulatory and executive powers of the state with respect to marine life.
Qualifications: The commission shall be composed of 7 members appointed by the governor, subject to confirmation by the senate.

Florida Citrus Commission

Authority: Section 601.04, Florida Statutes
Term: 3 years
Confirmation Required: Senate
Oversight: Department of Citrus
Compensation: $25.00 for each day of service + per diem, in accordance with Section 112.061 of the Florida Statutes
Description: The commission serves as head of the Department of Citrus and executes all functions vested in the department. The commission makes policy decisions on details not in the adopted marketing order.

Qualifications: Members shall be residents of Florida who have derived most of their income for at least 5 years from the growing, shipping and growing, or processing and growing of citrus fruit. There shall be 7 grower members and 5 grower-handler members. See the Florida Statutes for more information.

Florida Forever Advisory Council

Authority: Section 259.0345, Florida Statutes
Term: 3 years
Confirmation Required: None
Oversight: Department of Environmental Protection
Compensation: $75.00 for each day of service + per diem, in accordance with Section 112.061 of the Florida Statutes
Description: The council makes recommendations for the development and identification of performance measures; these measures are used to analyze the progress made toward the goals which have been established by the Forever Florida Act. The council provides recommendations for the process by which projects are to be submitted, reviewed, and approved by the Acquisition and Restoration Council.
Qualifications: The council shall consist of 7 members appointed by the governor. The chair is appointed by the governor. Members from the water management districts must have resided in the district for at least 1 year. Members shall represent the "development community," local government, etc.

Florida Greenways and Trails Council

Authority: Section 260.0142, Florida Statutes
Term: 2 years
Confirmation Required: None
Oversight: Department of Environmental Protection
Compensation: Per diem, in accordance with Section 112.061 of the Florida Statutes
Description: The council advises the Department of Environmental Protection and other agencies on policies relating to the

Florida Greenways and Trails System, promotes intergovernmental cooperation, recommends priorities for critical links in the Florida Greenways and Trail System, and facilitate a statewide system for interconnected land-based trails that connect urban, suburban, and rural areas of the state.

Qualifications: The council shall be composed of 21 members, 5 appointed by the governor. No member shall serve on the council for more than 2 consecutive terms.

Florida Inland Navigation District

Authority: Section 374.983, Florida Statutes
Term: 4 years
Confirmation Required: Senate
Oversight: Department of Environmental Protection
Compensation: Per diem, in accordance with Section 112.061 of the Florida Statutes
Description: The board performs and does all things requisite and necessary to comply with the requirements and conditions imposed upon a "local interest" by the congress of the United States, in the several acts authorizing and directing the improvement and maintenance of the Intercoastal Waterway from St. Mary's River, to the southernmost boundary of Dade County.
Qualifications: The board of commissioners shall be composed of 11 members appointed by the governor and subject to senate confirmation. Only 1 member shall be from each of the following counties: Duval, St. Johns, Flagler, Volusia, Brevard, St. Lucie, Martin, India River, Palm Beach, Broward, and Dade.

Florida Institute of Phosphate Research

Authority: Section 378.101, Florida Statutes
Term: 3 years
Confirmation Required: None
Oversight: Department of Environmental Protection

Compensation: Per diem, in accordance with Section 112.061 of the Florida Statutes
Description: The institute conducts environmental studies related to water consumption, radiation, and other environmental effects of phosphate mining and reclamation.
Qualifications: The governor shall appoint 5 members. One shall be from the faculty of a state university, one from a major conservation group, 1 from state government, and 2 from the phosphate mining or processing industry.

Florida Keys Aqueduct Authority

Authority: Chapter 76-441, Amended 84-484, Laws of Florida
Term: 4 years
Confirmation Required: None
Oversight: County Jurisdiction
Compensation: Per diem, in accordance with Section 112.061 of the Florida Statutes
Description: The authority creates and improves water systems for the Florida Keys, and regulates the use and supply of water, including rationing and regulations to enforce rationing.
Qualifications: Five regular members shall be appointed by governor. They shall be registered electors who have resided in Monroe County for at least 6 months.

Florida Panther Technical Advisory Council

Authority: Section 372.673, Florida Statutes
Term: 4 years
Confirmation Required: None
Oversight: Game and Fresh Water Fish Commission
Compensation: Per diem, in accordance with Section 112.061 of the Florida Statutes
Description: The council advises the Game and Fresh Water Fish Commission about the Florida Panther Recovery Program. The council reviews research and management programs which might cause harm to panthers. The council provides a forum for discussion of the Florida Panther Recovery Program.

Qualifications: The council shall consist of 7 members appointed by the governor. Members shall have technical knowledge and expertise in the research and management of large mammals.

Gulf of Mexico Program Citizens Advisory Committee

Authority: Federal EPA laws
Term: Pleasure of the Governor
Confirmation Required: None
Oversight: Federal Organization Titles
Compensation: Per diem, in accordance with Section 112.061 of the Florida Statutes
Description: The committee is part of the Gulf of Mexico Program to develop a management plan to protect and enhance the environmental and economic resources of the Gulf of Mexico, its estuaries, and its wetlands.
Qualifications: Each governor from the states participating in this program shall appoint 5 members from his or her state, each representing one these 5 interests: agriculture, fisheries, tourism, business/industry, and the environment.

Gulf States Marine Fisheries Commission

Authority: Section 370.20(2) Florida Statutes
Term: 3 years
Confirmation Required: Senate
Oversight: Department of Environmental Protection
Compensation: Per diem, in accordance with Section 112.061 of the Florida Statutes
Description: The commission ascertains such methods, practices, and conditions as may be disclosed for bringing about the conservation and prevention of the depletion and waste of Gulf Seaboard fisheries.

Qualifications: The citizen member shall be appointed by the governor. Members shall have a knowledge of and an interest in the marine fisheries.

Jupiter Inlet District, Palm Beach County

Authority: Chapter 81-458, Laws of Florida
Term: 4 years
Confirmation Required: None
Oversight: County Jurisdiction
Compensation: Per diem, in accordance with Section 112.061 of the Florida Statutes
Description: The district maintains an inlet connecting the mouth of the Jupiter River with the Atlantic Ocean.
Qualifications: Members shall be resident property owners. The governor shall appoint vacancies. Members shall post bond before assuming office.

Marine Fisheries Management Councils (Federal): South Atlantic and Gulf of Mexico Fishery Management Council

Authority: Chapter 16, U.S. Constitution Section 1801
Term: 3 years
Confirmation Required: None
Oversight: Federal Organization Titles
Compensation: Per diem, in accordance with Section 112.061 of the Florida Statutes
Description: These councils have been created by the Magnuson Fishery Conservation and Management Act, Chapter 16 of the U.S. Constitution, Section 1801and are comprised of representatives from North and South Carolina, Georgia, and Florida. A member from Florida is selected pursuant to 302(b) of the Magnuson Act.
Qualifications: There shall be 3 commissioners representing the South Atlantic Fishery Management Council, and 3 commissioners representing the Gulf of Mexico Fishery Management Council. The governor shall be prohibited from nominating anyone who has been a lobbyist of the industry within the last 24 months.

Miami River Coordinating Committee

Authority: County Resolution 1114-86
Term: Pleasure of the Governor
Confirmation Required:
Oversight: Federal Organization Titles
Compensation: Per diem, in accordance with Section 112.061 of the Florida Statutes
Description: The committee acts as a clearinghouse of information for citizens needing assistance regarding any of the various agencies having jurisdiction over the river, as well as other functions listed in the resolute.
Qualifications: Two of the governor's appointees shall have demonstrated an interest in the protection and enhancement of the Miami River, shall not be elected officials or state employees, and shall represent a cross-section of citizens.

Nongame Wildlife Advisory Council

Authority: Section 372.992, Florida Statutes
Term: 4 years
Confirmation Required: None
Oversight: Fish and Wildlife Conservation Commission
Compensation: Per diem, in accordance with Section 112.061 of the Florida Statutes
Description: The council recommends policies, objectives, and specific actions for non-game wildlife research and management to the Fish and Wildlife Conservation Commission.
Qualifications: The council shall consist of 11 members appointed by the governor. All appointments shall be for 4 year terms. Members shall be eligible for reappointment.

Nonmandatory Land Reclamation Committee

Authority: Section 378.33, Florida Statutes
Term: 4 years
Confirmation Required: Cabinet

Oversight: Department of Environmental Protection
Compensation: Per diem, in accordance with Section 112.061 of the Florida Statutes
Description: The committee reviews requests to fund reclamation projects of nonmandatory land (land mined for phosphate prior to July 1, 1975). The committee ranks the projects for approval by the governor and cabinet. This is an advisory body appointed by the governor and approved by the Cabinet.
Qualifications: There shall be 5 members on this board, and they should provide the program with engineering, fiscal, reclamation, and environmental expertise. Three members shall be elected respectively from Hamilton County, Polk County and Hillsborough County.

Pesticide Review Council

Authority: Section 487.0615, Florida Statutes
Term: 4 years
Confirmation Required: None
Oversight: Department of Agriculture and Consumer Changes
Compensation: Per diem, in accordance with Section 112.061 of the Florida Statutes
Description: The council reviews EPA data on any pesticides. It initiates studies on registered pesticides that appear to be a threat to environmental or human health, or that appear to make false claims in registration application.
Qualifications: The governor shall appoint 6 of the 7 scientific members.

Regional Marine Research Board—Gulf of Mexico

Authority: Federal Law 101-593
Term: 4 years
Confirmation Required: None
Oversight: County Jurisdiction
Compensation: Per diem, in accordance with Section 112.061 of the Florida Statutes

Description: A regional marine research board has been established for the Gulf of Mexico region, comprised of the marine and coastal waters off the states of Florida, Alabama, Mississippi, Louisiana, and Texas along the Gulf coast, is focused on marine research and management from the Florida Keys to the Mexican Border.

Qualifications: Members shall possess expertise in scientific research, coastal zone management, fishery management, water quality management, and state and local government. A majority of members shall be trained in a field of marine or aqua science and shall be currently engaged in research.

River Basin Boards (9): Alafia, Big Cypress, Coastal, Hillsborough, Manasota, Northwest Hillsborough, Peace, Pinellas-Anclote, and Withlacoochee River

Authority: Section 373.0693, Florida Statutes
Term: 3 years
Confirmation Required: Senate
Oversight: Department of Environmental Protection
Compensation: Per diem, in accordance with Section 112.061 of the Florida Statutes
Description: These boards prepare water resource and control facility plans; approve construction of works in the river basin, and plan water supply transmission. These boards are administered by the water management districts.
Qualifications: The boards shall consist of not less than 3 members, and shall include one representative from each of the counties. See the Florida Statutes for details.

Small Business Air Pollution Compliance Advisory Council

Authority: Section 403.8051, Florida Statutes
Term: 4 years
Confirmation Required: None
Oversight: Department of Environmental Protection

Compensation: Per diem, in accordance with Section 112.061 of the Florida Statutes
Description: The council renders advice on the effectiveness of the department's small business stationary air pollution source technical and environmental assistance program, the difficulties encountered, and the degree and severity of enforcement. The council also makes periodic reports to the administrator of the U.S. Environmental Protection Agency.
Qualifications: The council shall consist of 7 members. Two members shall be appointed by the governor. Members shall not be owners or representatives of owners of small business stationary sources.

Southeast Interstate Low-Level Radioactive Waste Management Commission

Authority: Section 404.30, Florida Statutes
Term: 2 years
Confirmation Required: Senate
Oversight: Department of Health
Compensation: Per diem, in accordance with Section 112.061 of the Florida Statutes
Description: The commission works within a regional low-level radioactive waste management compact, for the purpose of providing sufficient facilities for the proper management of low-level radioactive waste.
Qualifications: The commission shall consist of 2 voting members from each state party to be appointed according to the laws of each state. Two alternates may act on behalf of the members only in their absence.

Water Advisory Panel

Authority: Executive Order 99-288
Term: 1 year
Confirmation Required: None

Oversight: Department of Environmental Protection
Compensation: Per diem, in accordance with Section 112.061 of the Florida Statutes
Description: The panel will accept applications for water projects in the 3 categories of wastewater, surface water, and storm water. The purpose of this panel is to enhance water resources that meet state water quality standards and support healthy natural ecosystems.
Qualifications: The Water Advisory Panel shall consist of 15 members. Five members shall be appointed by the governor, 5 by the Speaker of the House, and 5 by the president of the Senate. Appointments to the panel shall be made by June 30 of each year, and shall take effect on July 1, for a term of 1 year.

Water Management District Governing Boards, (3): Northwest, Southwest, and South Florida; and River Water Management District Governing Board (2): St. Johns and Suwannee River

Authority: Section 373.073, Florida Statutes
Term: 4 years
Confirmation Required: Senate
Oversight: Department of Environmental Protection
Compensation: Per diem, in accordance with Section 112.061 of the Florida Statutes
Description: Each board issues orders implementing or enforcing the provisions relating to the use and consumption of the water resources of Florida. They discharge the functions as set by the legislature; conserve, protect, manage, and control state waters, preserve natural resources, fish and wildlife, and promote recreational protection. The board establishes saltwater barrier lines, surveys and investigates water resources, determines areas for groundwater basin resource, and sets guidelines for flow of watercourses and water level. The board conducts surveys of water resources and establishes guidelines for surface water sources and water levels, levies taxes to finance basin functions, and plans to meet water supply level needs.

Qualifications: The governor shall appoint 11 members, according to residency requirements prescribed in the Florida Statutes. Members shall subscribe to an oath of office. The appointment of an executive director must be initially confirmed by the Florida Senate. No county shall have more than 3 members on each board, and no more than one at-large member shall be from the same county. One member from each hydrological unit in the district and 4 at large representatives.

Waterfowl Advisory Council

Authority: Section 372.5714, Florida Statutes
Term: 4 years
Confirmation Required: None
Oversight: Game and Fresh Water Fish Commission
Compensation: Per diem, in accordance with Section 112.061 of the Florida Statutes
Description: The council consults with and advises the Game and Freshwater Fish Commission on the establishment and operation of projects for the protection and propagation of migratory waterfowl and wetlands.
Qualifications: Members shall be representatives of appropriate state agencies or conservation groups, or private citizens who possess knowledge and experience in waterfowl management and protection.

Arts / Entertainment / Tourism

The boards, commissions and senior level appointments listed in this chapter encourage the arts, foster cultural programs, and stimulate the study or presentation of the arts. They help to enhance the interiors of the Capitol Building and other public buildings. They make recommendations for cultural grant funding, and plan and implement programs designed to gain national and international recognition on behalf of Florida artists. People selected for these appointments also help to ensure that Florida is a world-renowned entertainment destination by developing, marketing, promoting, and providing service to Florida's entertainment industry. They work with the legislature, state agencies, business leaders, and economic development professionals to formulate strategies that will keep Florida's tourism economy strong. Appointed by the governor, the secretary of state serves as the Chief Cultural Officer of Florida (among other duties), and in turn he or she appoints the Director of the Division of Cultural Affairs.

Senior Level Appointments:

Secretary of the Department of State

Secretary of the Department of Lottery

State Film Commissioner

Director of the Governor's Mansion

Chair of the Florida Arts Council

Boards and Commissions:

Board of Directors, Florida Sports Foundation

Authority: Section 288.1229, Florida Statutes
Term: 4 years
Confirmation Required: None
Oversight: Office of Tourism, Trade and Economic Development
Compensation: Per diem, in accordance with Section 112.061 of the Florida Statutes
Description: The directors benefit the council and act in the best interests of the state as a direct-support organization to the council. They receive, hold, invest, and administer property to raise funds, receive gifts, and promote and develop professional sports and related industry.
Qualifications: The governor shall appoint 15 members to the board of directors. Appointees shall be residents of the state and highly knowledgeable of, or active in, professional sports. No member shall serve more than 2 consecutive terms.

Daytona Beach Racing and Recreational Facilities Commission

Authority: Chapter 55-31343, Laws of Florida
Term: 4 years
Confirmation Required: None

Oversight: County Jurisdiction
Compensation: Per diem, in accordance with Section 112.061 of the Florida Statutes
Description: The commission adopts bylaws for the regulation of its affairs and the conduct of its business, and purchases or otherwise acquires, constructs, reconstructs, improves, extends, enlarges, equips, repairs, maintains, and operates any racing and recreational facilities within the territorial limits of the district.
Qualifications: The commission shall consist of 5 members. The county and city commission each shall appoint 2 members. The 2 commissions shall appoint one member jointly. If the commissions cannot agree on the joint appointee, the governor shall make the appointment.

Dr. Martin Luther King, Jr. Commemorative Commission

Authority: Executive Order 92-199
Term: 2 years
Confirmation Required: None
Oversight: Office of the Governor
Compensation: Per diem, in accordance with Section 112.061 of the Florida Statutes
Description: The commission coordinates, promotes and reviews plans for the celebration of Dr. Martin Luther King, Jr.'s birthday. The commission consults with the Department of Education and other state agencies to develop educational material and publications that will represent the life and works of Dr. King and magnify a respect for the bequest left by Dr. King.
Qualifications: The commission shall consist of no more than 21 members appointed by the governor. The governor appoints the chairperson.

Fiesta of Five Flags Commission of Pensacola

Authority: Chapter 65-2098, Laws of Florida
Term: 3 years
Confirmation Required: None

Oversight: County Jurisdiction
Compensation: Per diem, in accordance with Section 112.061 of the Florida Statutes
Description: The commission stages public celebrations, fiestas, pageants, parades, contests, races, and other entertainment features for the citizens of the city of Pensacola and their guests.
Qualifications: Members shall not be employees of the city of Pensacola. The governor shall appoint 3 members to the commission.

Florida Arts Council

Authority: Section 265.285, Florida Statutes
Term: 4 years
Confirmation Required: None
Oversight: Department of State
Compensation: Per diem, in accordance with Section 112.061 of the Florida Statutes
Description: The council advises the secretary of state in all matters pertaining to art, stimulates and encourage the study and presentation of the arts, as well as public interest and participation throughout the state, and promotes the enhancement of the interiors of the Capitol Building and other public buildings, along with advising appropriate state officials, state agencies and the Department of Management Services
Qualifications: The council shall consist of 15 members, 7 appointed by the governor. No member shall serve more than two 4 year terms. Members shall have a substantial history of community service in the performing or visual arts, including theater, dance, folk arts, music, etc.

Florida Commission of Tourism

Authority: Section 288.1223, Florida Statutes
Term: 4 years
Confirmation Required: Senate
Oversight: Office of Tourism, Trade and Economic Development

Compensation: Per diem, in accordance with Section 112.061 of the Florida Statutes

Description: The commission is established to increase the positive impact of tourism, and to promote tourism to upgrade the image of Florida. The commission also advises on the creation of objectives for all geographic, socio-economic, and community sectors considered equitably. Its efforts are judged by the same standards of accountability and integrity as those used by successful, respected private sector businesses.

Qualifications: The governor shall appoint 27 general tourism- industry related members. The members shall be appointed to represent all geographic areas of the state.

Florida Film and Entertainment Advisory Council

Authority: Section 288.1252, Florida Statutes
Term: 4 years
Confirmation Required: None
Oversight: Office of Tourism, Trade and Economic Development
Compensation: Per diem, in accordance with Section 112.061 of the Florida Statutes
Description: The council serves as an advisory body to the Office of Tourism, Trade and Economic Development, and to the Office of the Film Commissioner to provide these offices with industry insight and expertise related to developing, marketing, promoting, and providing service to the state's entertainment industry.
Qualifications: The council shall consist of 17 members, 7 appointed by the governor. No more than one member may be from any company. Members are limited to 2 consecutive terms. Members may be removed for missing 3 consecutive meetings.

Florida Historical Commission

Authority: Section 267.0612, Florida Statutes
Term: 4 years
Confirmation Required: None

Oversight: Department of State
Compensation: Per diem, in accordance with Section 112.061 of the Florida Statutes
Description: The commission establishs priorities for the protection and the preservation of historical and archaeological sites and properties. The members serve as the legislative historic preservation advisory body, with respect to the collection and preservation of the historic records of both houses of the state legislature.
Qualifications: The commission shall consist of 11 members, 7 appointed by the governor in consultation with the secretary of state. The senate president and the Speaker shall each appoint 2 members. At least one member shall be a resident of a county with a population of 75,000 or less.

Florida Humanities Council

Authority: Section 501 Chapter 3 U.S. IRC
Term: 4 years
Confirmation Required: None
Oversight: Federal Organization Titles
Compensation: Per diem, in accordance with Section 112.061 of the Florida Statutes
Description: The endowment supports activities which foster public knowledge and appreciation of the humanities, and which strengthen the bond between the humanities and the people of Florida.
Qualifications: Members shall come from a wide cross section of Floridians and must be committed to promoting the goals of the endowment. Members' tenure in office shall coincide with the governor's tenure in office.

Florida State Boxing Commission

Authority: Section 548-003, Florida Statutes
Term: 4 years
Confirmation Required: Senate
Oversight: Department of Business and Professional Regulation

Compensation: Per diem, in accordance with Section 112.061 of the Florida Statutes
Description: The commission has exclusive jurisdiction over professional boxing matches held in the State; establishes rules, boxing weights, classes, and fees, and decides such issues as cancellation of matches.
Qualifications: There are no specific qualifications stated. The governor shall appoint the first chairperson. Thereafter, the commission shall select a chairperson following June 1 of each year.

Governor's Mansion Commission

Authority: Section 272.18, Florida Statutes
Term: 4 years
Confirmation Required: Senate
Oversight: Department of Environmental Protection
Compensation: Per diem, in accordance with Section 112.061 of the Florida Statutes
Description: This commission is responsible for the maintenance of the governor's mansion, the grounds, furniture, and all fixtures. The commission adopts rules governing the use of the mansion and also recommends any structural changes.
Qualifications: Members shall not hold any other state or local office and are subject to removal from office if guilty of a felony. The spouse of the governor or a designated representative shall serve as an ex officio member.

Hillsborough County Law Library Board

Authority: Chapter 65-832, Laws of Florida
Term: 4 years
Confirmation Required: None
Oversight: County Jurisdiction
Compensation: Per diem, in accordance with Section 112.061 of the Florida Statutes

Description: The library board has the power to buy, sell, exchange, or receive donations of books and law journals. The board also maintains a law library for the use of the district.

Qualifications: The directors shall be members of the county bar in good professional standing and of high moral character. Nominations for appointments shall come from the county bar associations.

Judah P. Benjamin Memorial at Gamble Plantation Historical Site Advisory Council

Authority: Section 258.155, Florida Statutes
Term: 4 years
Confirmation Required: None
Oversight: Department of Environmental Protection
Compensation: Per diem, in accordance with Section 112.061 of the Florida Statutes
Description: The council advises the Division of Recreation and Parks, a subdivision of the Department of Environmental Protection in its role in the operation, restoration, developments and preservation of the Gamble Plantation Memorial.
Qualifications: Members shall be citizens and residents of Manatee County. Three members shall be appointed from the membership of the United Daughters of the Confederacy, 1 member shall be appointed from the Manatee County Historical Society, and 1 member shall be appointed at large from Manatee County.

Merritt Island Library District Board, Brevard County

Authority: Chapter 65-1289, Laws of Florida
Term: 3 years
Confirmation Required: None
Oversight: County Jurisdiction
Compensation: Per diem, in accordance with Section 112.061 of the Florida Statutes

Description: The board maintains and conducts a library, as well as any facilities, buildings, and structures related to and used or operated in conjunction with a library.
Qualifications: Members shall be property owners in the district. Members must reside within the Merritt Island boundary.

Nature-Based and Heritage Tourism Advisory Committee

Authority: Section 288.1224, Florida Statutes
Term: 4 years
Confirmation Required: None
Oversight: Office of Tourism, Trade and Economic Development
Compensation: Per diem, in accordance with Section 112.061 of the Florida Statutes
Description: The advisory committee is established to assist the tourism commission with implementation of a plan to protect and promote all of the natural, coastal, historical, and cultural tourism assets of the state. The committee helps to develop and review nature-based tourism and heritage tourism policies. It also coordinates governmental and private-sector interests in nature- based tourism.
Qualifications: The governor, who is the chairperson of the tourism commission, shall appoint members of the advisory committee, based upon recommendations from the tourism commission.

State Historical Records Advisory Board

Authority: Section 65.203, Florida Statutes
Term: 3 years
Confirmation Required: None
Oversight: Federal Organization Titles
Compensation: Per diem, in accordance with Section 112.061 of the Florida Statutes
Description: The advisory board serves as the state's central advisory body for historical records. The board also reviews grant applications submitted to the National Historical Records and

Publications Commission. As a guide for its work, the board assesses conditions and needs of the historical records' programs in the state and establishes funding priorities.

Qualifications: Member of the board shall be appointed by the governor. The majority of the members must have some recognized experience in the administration of government records, historical records, or archives.

Tampa Sports Authority

Authority: Chapter 96-520, Laws of Florida
Term: 4 years
Confirmation Required: None
Oversight: County Jurisdiction
Compensation: Per diem, in accordance with Section 112.061 of the Florida Statutes
Description: Authority members plan, develop, and maintain a comprehensive complex of sports and recreation facilities for the use and enjoyment of the citizens of Tampa and Hillsborough County.
Qualifications: Members shall take an oath of office. The governor shall appoint only one member. Four members shall be appointed by the mayor and 4 by the county commission. One city councilman and 1 county commissioner shall be ex officio.

Business /
Economic Development /
Workforce Innovation

The boards, commissions and senior level appointments listed in this chapter are responsible for protecting the public's health, safety, and welfare, by ensuring that regulated businesses, industries, and professionals meet certain standards of education and competency. Business and industry regulations include the manufacture, distribution, and retail sale of alcoholic beverages and tobacco products; public lodgings and food services; the sale of subdivided lands, condominiums, and cooperatives, real estate time shares, and mobile home parks; yacht and ship brokerages; and health service pools, to name a few. Also, some 27 professions, such as accountants, building contractors, realtors, architects, land surveyors, and cosmetologists, are regulated by the various boards and commissions listed. In an effort to advance Florida's economic prosperity, these boards and commissions assist our workforce by providing innovative, timely, and accurate business support services. They also implement policies that deal with workforce development programs, welfare transition, and unemployment compensation. They assist the governor in working with the legislature, state agencies, business leaders, and others to formulate policies and strategies designed to provide economic opportunities for all Floridians.

Senior level appointments:

Secretary of the Department of Business & Professional Regulation

Secretary of the Department of Labor and Employment Security

Director of the Agency for Workforce Innovation

Director of the Office of Tourism, Trade, and Economic Development

Commissioner of Deeds for the State of Florida

Chair of the Public Employee Relations Commission

Chair of the Unemployment Appeals Commission

Boards and Commissions:

Barbers Board

Authority: Section 460.404, Florida Statutes
Term: 4 years
Confirmation Require: Senate
Oversight: Department of Business and Professional Regulation
Compensation: $50.00 per day of service + per diem, in accordance with Section 112.061 of the Florida Statutes
Description: The board sets licensing fees and requirements, as well as specifying areas of competency for examination. The board prescribes continuing educational requirements, and revokes or suspends licenses for due cause.
Qualifications: Members shall not be connected with the manufacture, rental, or wholesale of barber supplies, or with a school of barbering. Members shall not serve more than 2 consecutive terms.

Board of Accountancy

Authority: Section 473.303, Florida Statutes

Term: 4 years
Confirmation Require: Senate
Oversight: Department of Business and Professional Regulation
Compensation: $50.00 per day of service + per diem, in accordance with Section 112.061 of the Florida Statutes
Description: The board sets licensing fees, establishes educational standards for licensure, and certifies qualified applicants and firms for licensure as certified public accountants.
Qualifications: The members who are certified public accountants shall have practiced public accounting on a substantially full-time basis for at least 5 years. Pursuant to Chapter 87-172 of the laws of Florida, at least 1 member shall be 60 years of age or older.

Board of Architecture and Interior Design

Authority: Section 481.205, Florida Statutes
Term: 4 years
Confirmation Require: Senate
Oversight: Department of Business and Professional Regulation
Compensation: $50.00 per day of service + per diem, in accordance with Section 112.061 of the Florida Statutes
Description: The board sets licensing fees and adopts rules relating to the examination, internship, and licensure of applicants. The board certifies all qualified applicants to the department of business and professional regulations in this area.
Qualifications: Five members shall be registered architects, 3 members shall be interior designers, and 3 members shall be consumers. Pursuant to Chapter 87-172 of the laws of Florida, at least 1 member shall be 60 years of age or older.

Board of Auctioneers

Authority: Section 468.384, Florida Statutes
Term: 4 years
Confirmation Required: Senate
Oversight: Department of Business and Professional Regulation

Compensation: $50.00 per day of service + per diem, in accordance with Section 112.061 of the Florida Statutes
Description: The board receives and acts upon applications for auctioneer, apprentice, and auction business licenses. It also has the power to issue, suspend, and revoke such licenses.
Qualifications: The members of each board (that has been established pursuant to subsection (4), (5), (6), and (7)), shall be appointed by the governor.

Board of Cosmetology

Authority: Section 477.015, Florida Statutes
Term: 4 years
Confirmation Require: Senate
Oversight: Department of Business and Professional Regulation
Compensation: $50.00 per day of service + per diem, in accordance with Section 112.061 of the Florida Statutes
Description: The board is authorized to establish educational standards and rules for licensure of practitioners, cosmetology instructors, schools, and salons, including competencies to be covered by examination.
Qualifications: Each board member shall have been a resident of Florida for 5 continuous years, shall serve no more than 2 consecutive terms, and shall take the constitutional oath of office.

Board of Directors, Enterprise Florida, Inc.

Authority: Section 288.901, Florida Statutes
Term: 4 years
Confirmation Required: Senate
Oversight: Office of Tourism, Trade, and Economic Development
Compensation: Per diem, in accordance with Section 112.061 of the Florida Statutes
Description: The board assists in the coordination of the state's economic development efforts, including the development of a stra-

tegic plan. The board secures funding for programs and activities of Enterprise Florida, Inc., from federal, state, local, and private sources. The board adopts, amends, and repeals bylaws. The board of directors shall appoint an executive director.

Qualifications: The governor shall appoint 6 of the 22 members. Absence from 3 consecutive meetings shall result in automatic removal. Membership shall reflect the diversity of Florida's business community. The governor shall serve as chairperson of the board of directors.

Board of Directors, Workforce Florida, Inc.

Authority: Section 445.004, Florida Statutes
Term: 2 years
Confirmation Required: None
Oversight: Agency for Workforce Innovation
Compensation: Per diem, in accordance with Section 112.061 of the Florida Statutes
Description: The board of directors designs and implements strategies that help Floridians enter, remain, and advance in the workplace, becoming more highly skilled and successful, thus benefitting these Floridians, Florida businesses, and the entire state's business climate.
Qualifications: The board shall be appointed by the governor. Absence from 3 consecutive meetings shall result in automatic removal. The importance of minority and gender representation shall be considered when making appointments to the board.

Board of Employee Leasing Companies

Authority: Section 468.521, Florida Statutes
Term: 4 years
Confirmation Required: Senate
Oversight: Department of Business and Professional Regulation
Compensation: $50.00 per day of service + per diem, in accordance with Section 112.061 of the Florida Statutes

Description: The board adopts all rules necessary to administer this act. Every licensee is governed and controlled by the act and the rules adopted by the board.
Qualifications: The board shall consist of 7 members appointed by the governor and confirmed by the senate. Five members shall engage in the employee leasing industry. The remaining 2 members shall be consumers.

Board of Funeral and Cemetery Services

Authority: Section 497.101, Florida Statutes
Term: 4 years
Confirmation Required: Senate
Oversight: Department of Banking and Finance
Compensation: Per diem, in accordance with Section 112.061 of the Florida Statutes
Description: The board is authorized to adopt rules, not inconsistent with law, as may be necessary to carry out the duties and authority conferred upon the board to protect the health, safety, and welfare of the public. The board adopts rules which establish requirements for inspection of cemeteries.
Qualifications: The board shall consist of 7 members appointed by the governor, who shall come from nominations made by the comptroller and confirmed by the senate. The comptroller shall nominate 3 persons for each vacancy on the board. At least 1 member of the board shall be 60 years of age or older.

Board of Funeral Directors and Embalmers

Authority: Section 470.003, Florida Statutes
Term: 4 years
Confirmation Require: Senate
Oversight: Department of Business and Professional Regulation
Compensation: $50.00 per day of service + per diem, in accordance with Section 112.061 of the Florida Statutes

Description: The board makes rules necessary to carry out the intent of Chapter 470 of the Florida Statutes regarding the licensing and registration of funeral directors, embalmers, and direct disposers.

Qualifications: Five members shall be licensed under Chapter 470 of the Florida Statutes, and 2 shall be lay members who are not connected with the practice of embalming or funeral directing. At least 1 consumer member of the board shall be 60 years of age or older.

Board of Landscape Architecture

Authority: Section 481.305, Florida Statutes
Term: 4 years
Confirmation Require: Senate
Oversight: Department of Business and Professional Regulation
Compensation: $50.00 per day of service + per diem, in accordance with Section 112.061 of the Florida Statutes
Description: The board establishs fees for examination and licensing, certifies qualified applicants, specifies grounds for disciplinary action, and reports any criminal violations of statutory provisions.
Qualifications: The board shall consist of 5 landscape architects and 2 lay members.

Board of Pilot Commissioners

Authority: Section 310.011, Florida Statutes
Term: 4 years
Confirmation Require: Senate
Oversight: Department of Business and Professional Regulation
Compensation: $50.00 per day of service + per diem, in accordance with Section 112.061 of the Florida Statutes
Description: The board performs duties relative to the protection of the waters, harbors, and ports of Florida, including the suspension of licenses and the setting of license fees for pilots conducting vessels.

Qualifications: No member shall serve more than 2 consecutive terms on the board.

Board of Professional Engineers

Authority: Section 471.007, Florida Statutes
Term: 4 years
Confirmation Require: Senate
Oversight: Department of Business and Professional Regulation
Compensation: $50.00 per day of service + per diem, in accordance with Section 112.061 of the Florida Statutes
Description: The board reviews and approves courses of study, certifies those who meet statutory requirements, and registers qualified applicants of a partnership or corporation.
Qualifications: No member shall serve more than 2 consecutive terms. Seven members shall be licensed engineers and 2 lay members shall be appointed by the governor.

Board of Professional Geologists

Authority: Section 492.103, Florida Statutes
Term: 4 years
Confirmation Required: Senate
Oversight: Department of Business and Professional Regulation
Compensation: $50.00 per day of service + per diem, in accordance with Section 112.061 of the Florida Statutes
Description: The board adopts rules for fee application, examination, certification, initial licensure, and license renewal for professional geologists.
Qualifications: The chief of the Bureau of Geology in the Department of Environmental Protection shall serve as an ex-officio member of the board. (See Amendment 88-492(1).

Board of Professional Surveyors and Mappers

Authority: Section 472.007, Florida Statutes
Term: 4 years

Confirmation Require: Senate
Oversight: Department of Business and Professional Regulation
Compensation: $50.00 per day of service + per diem, in accordance with Section 112.061 of the Florida Statutes
Description: The board sets fees for licensing and examination, provides for the approval of schools and courses of study, establishes minimum technical standards, and certifies qualified applicants for land surveyor.
Qualifications: Members shall include 6 registered land surveyors and mappers, one photogrammetric mapper, and 2 lay members. They shall serve 4 year terms.

Board of Veterinary Medicine

Authority: Section 474.204, Florida Statutes
Term: 4 years
Confirmation Require: Senate
Oversight: Department of Business and Professional Regulation
Compensation: $50.00 per day of service + per diem, in accordance with Section 112.061 of the Florida Statutes
Description: The board certifies qualified applicants, sets standards for approval of veterinary schools, imposes penalties for disciplinary cases, and sets standards on conditions for veterinary establishments.
Qualifications: Five members shall be licensed veterinarians and 2 shall be lay members.

Child Care Executive Partnership

Authority: Section 409.178(4), Florida Statutes
Term: 4 years
Confirmation Required: None
Oversight: Agency for Workforce Innovation
Compensation: Per diem, in accordance with Section 112.061 of the Florida Statutes
Description: The Child Care Executive Partnership (CCEP) establishes and governs the child care partnership program. The purpose of the program is to utilize state and federal funds as incentives for matching local funds derived from local government

employers, charitable foundations, and other sources, so that Florida communities may create local flexible partnerships with employers.
Qualifications: The board shall consist of 10 members appointed by the governor, including a representative of the executive office of the governor. The other 9 members shall be from the corporate or childcare community.

Construction Industry Licensing Board

Authority: Section 489.107, Florida Statutes
Term: 4 years
Confirmation Required: Senate
Oversight: Department of Business and Professional Regulation
Compensation: $50.00 per day of service + per diem, in accordance with Section 112.061 of the Florida Statutes
Description: The board adopts by rule, procedures for the certification of contractors, licensing fees, and limits for liability insurance to be maintained by the contractor.
Qualifications: Eighteen members shall be appointed by the governor. Members shall not serve more than 2 consecutive 4 year terms, nor serve for more than 11 years on the board.

Council of Economic Advisors

Authority: Executive Order 02-317
Term: December 31, 2004
Confirmation Required: None
Oversight: Office of Tourism, Trade, and Economic Development
Compensation: Per diem, in accordance with Section 112.061 of the Florida Statutes
Description: The Council studies and makes recommendations about the impact of various economic issues upon the different sectors of Florida's economy, the relationship of the issue to national and global trends acting upon Florida's economy, and the likely future impact of issues on Florida's overall economy.

Qualifications: The council shall be composed of up to 13 members appointed by the governor. The chairperson shall be selected by the governor.

Electrical Contractors Licensing Board

Authority: Section 489.507, Florida Statutes
Term: 4 years
Confirmation Require: Senate
Oversight: Department of Business and Professional Regulation
Compensation: $50.00 per day of service + per diem, in accordance with Section 112.061 of the Florida Statutes
Description: The board adopts licensing rules and administers licensing requirements; investigates applicants and certifies qualified applicants and business organizations
Qualifications: Seven members of the board shall be certified electrical contractors, 2 shall be lay members, and 2 shall be certified alarm system contractors.

Florida Black Business Investment Board

Authority: Section 288.707, Florida Statutes
Term: 4 years
Confirmation Required: Senate
Oversight: Office of Tourism, Trade, and Economic Development
Compensation: Per diem, in accordance with Section 112.061 of the Florida Statutes
Description: The board works to strengthen the economy of the state by increasing qualified black business enterprises, increasing marketplace competition, and improving the welfare of economically depressed neighborhoods.
Qualifications: Six members of the board shall be experienced in investment finance and business development. Initial appointments shall be as follows: 1 member shall be appointed for 1 year; 2 members for 2 years; 2 members for 3 years; 2 members for 4 years. The governor shall appoint the chairperson.

Florida Building Code Administrators and Inspectors Board

Authority: Section 468.605, Florida Statutes
Term: 4 years
Confirmation Required: Senate
Oversight: Department of Business and Professional Regulation
Compensation: $50.00 per day of service + per diem, in accordance with Section 112.061 of the Florida Statutes
Description: The board adopts rules as necessary to carry out the provisions of this law. The board also certifies individuals as being qualified under the provisions of this law to be building code administrators, plans examiners, and building code inspectors.
Qualifications: The board shall consist of 9 members appointed by the governor and subject to senate confirmation. Members shall not serve more than 2 consecutive 4 year terms, nor serve for more than 11 years on the board.

Florida Building Commission

Authority: Section 533.74, Florida Statutes
Term: 4 years
Confirmation Require: Senate
Oversight: Department of Community Affairs
Compensation: Per diem, in accordance with Section 112.061 of the Florida Statutes
Description: The board makes a continual study of the state minimum building codes and other laws relating to the construction of buildings, as well as advising on new technologies and construction material.
Qualifications: Members shall not be engaged in the manufacture, promotion, or sale of any building materials.

Florida Development Finance Corporation

Authority: Section 288.9604, Florida Statutes
Term: 4 years
Confirmation Required: Senate

Oversight: Office of Tourism, Trade, and Economic Development
Compensation: Per diem, in accordance with Section 112.061 of the Florida Statutes
Description: The corporation is authorized and empowered to have perpetual succession as a political and corporate body, and to adopt bylaws for the regulation of its affairs and the conduct of its business.
Qualifications: The board of directors shall consist of 5 members who are appointed by the governor and subject to senate confirmation. At least 3 directors shall be bankers selected from a list nominated by the Enterprise Florida Partnership, and one director shall be an economic development specialist.

Florida Partnership for School Readiness

Authority: Section 411.01(4) Florida Statutes
Term: 4 years
Confirmation Required: None
Oversight: Agency for Workforce Innovation
Compensation: Per diem, in accordance with Section 112.061 of the Florida Statutes
Description: The Florida Partnership for School Readiness is the principal organization responsible for the enhancement of school readiness for the state's children, and it shall be responsible for the prudent use of all public and private funds. The partnership may develop and implement specific strategies that address the state's school readiness programs.
Qualifications: The partnership shall consist of 20 members, 14 who are appointed by the governor. Members shall be business, community, and civic leaders, and they must not have a direct contract with any coalition to provide school readiness services. The president and the Speaker shall submit a list of nominees.

Florida Real Estate Appraisal Board

Authority: Section 475.613, Florida Statutes
Term: 4 years

Confirmation Required: Senate
Oversight: Department of Business and Professional Regulation
Compensation: $50.00 per day of service + per diem, in accordance with Section 112.061 of the Florida Statutes
Description: The board has, through its rules, full power to regulate the issuance of licenses, certifications, registrations, and permits; to discipline appraisers in any manner permitted under this section; to establish qualifications for licenses, certifications, registrations, and permits; and to regulate approved courses and establish standards of appraisals.
Qualifications: Two members shall be licensed or certified residential appraisers, and 2 members shall be certified general real estate appraisers. One member shall represent an organization that uses appraisals for eminent domain, etc. Two members of the board shall be of the general public.

Florida Real Estate Commission

Authority: Section 475.02, Florida Statutes
Term: 4 years
Confirmation Require: Senate
Oversight: Department of Business and Professional Regulation
Compensation: $50.00 per day of service + per diem, in accordance with Section 112.061 of the Florida Statutes
Description: The board certifies those qualified to work as a broker or salesperson, registers each partnership or corporation acting as a broker, and prescribes continuing educational requirements and rules for records.
Qualifications: The commission shall consist of 5 professional members, as specified in Florida Statute 475.02(1), and 2 lay members. Pursuant to Chapter 87-172 of the laws of Florida, at least 1 member shall be 60 years of age or older.

Governor's Advisory Council on Farm Workers Affairs

Authority: Executive Order 96-138
Term: Pleasure of the Governor

Confirmation Required: None

Oversight: Department of Health

Compensation: Per diem, in accordance with Section 112.061 of the Florida Statutes

Description: The council is authorized and empowered to perform a catalytic role in state government, providing recommendations designed to bring solutions to farm worker problems and also working cooperatively with state officials to complement improvement efforts. The council makes all inquiries necessary to ascertain the manner by which governmental services may be enhanced in relationship to farm workers.

Qualifications: The council shall be composed of agriculture employers and farm workers, private groups, public agencies, and citizens at large, to be appointed by the governor. Members shall continue to serve at the pleasure of the governor.

Pilotage Rate Review Board

Authority: Section 310.151, Florida Statutes

Term: 4 years

Confirmation Required: Senate

Oversight: Department of Business and Professional Regulation

Compensation: $50.00 per day of service + per diem, in accordance with Section 112.061 of the Florida Statutes

Description: The board investigates and determines whether the requested rate change will result in fair, just, and reasonable rates of pilotage, pursuant to rules prescribed by the board. The board has the authority to set, by rule, a rate review application fee of up to $1,000.

Qualifications: The board shall consist of 7 members who are appointed by the governor and subject to confirmation by the senate. Members shall not serve more than 2 consecutive 4 year terms, nor serve for more than 11 years on the board. No member shall have ever served as a state pilot or deputy pilot.

Public Employee Optional Retirement Program Advisory Committee

Authority: Section 121.4501(12)(b), Florida Statutes
Term: 2 years
Confirmation Required: None
Oversight: Department of Management Services
Compensation: Per diem, in accordance with Section 112.061 of the Florida Statutes
Description: The advisory committee makes recommendations on the selection of the third-party administrator, the educational providers, and the investment products and providers.
Qualifications: The advisory committee shall consist of 7 members, 1 appointed by the governor, 1 by the comptroller, and 1 by the treasurer. The president of the senate and the Speaker of the House shall each appoint 2 members.

Public Employees Relations Commission

Authority: Section 447.205, Florida Statutes
Term: 4 years
Confirmation Require: Senate
Oversight: Department of Management Services
Compensation: $85,683.00 per year + per diem, in accordance with Section 112.061 of the Florida Statutes.
Description: The commission interprets and enforces the statutes and rules under which public employees may bargain collectively with their employers, determines bargaining units, and provides a forum for controversies.
Qualifications: Commissioners shall not be employed by or hold any commission with any governmental unit in the state or any employee organization, or engage in any other business or employment while in office.

Recycled Markets Advisory Committee

Authority: Section 288.1185, Florida Statutes

Term: Pleasure of the Governor
Confirmation Required: None
Oversight: Office of Tourism, Trade, and Economic Development
Compensation: Per diem, in accordance with Section 112.061 of the Florida Statutes
Description: The committee serves as the mechanism for coordination among state agencies and the private sector, coordinating policy and overall strategy planning for developing new markets, and expanding and enhancing existing markets for recovered materials. The committee may not duplicate or replace agency programs, but enhances, coordinates, and recommends priorities for those programs.
Qualifications: The board shall consist of 12 members, 10 appointed by the governor, each of whom is or has been actively engaged in the recycling industry or a related business area, or is a local government official with a demonstrated knowledge of recycling. The chairperson shall be appointed by the governor.

Regulatory Council of Community Association Managers

Authority: Section 468.4315, Florida Statutes
Term: 4 years
Confirmation Required: Senate
Oversight: Department of Business and Professional Regulation
Compensation: $50.00 per day of service + per diem, in accordance with Section 112.061 of the Florida Statutes
Description: The council may adopt rules relating to the licensure examination, continuing educational requirements, and fees and professional practice standards, in order to assist in carrying out the duties and authorities conferred upon the department.
Qualifications: The council shall consist of 7 members appointed by the governor and subject to senate confirmation. Five members shall be licensed community association managers, one of whom shall be employed by a timeshare managing entity. Two shall be lay members.

State Apprenticeship Council Nominating Committee

Authority: Section 446.045, Florida Statutes
Term: Pleasure of the Governor
Confirmation Required: None
Oversight: Department of Labor and Employment Security
Compensation: Per diem, in accordance with Section 112.061 of the Florida Statutes
Description: The council is advisory to the Department of Labor and Employment Security on matters governing the terms and conditions of the apprentice's employment and training.
Qualifications: Ten members shall be appointed by the governor. The members shall represent industries having registered apprenticeship programs, or in which a need for apprenticeship programs has been demonstrated.

State Innovation Committee

Authority: Section 216.235(4), Florida Statutes
Term: 1 year
Confirmation Required: None
Oversight: Office of Tourism, Trade, and Economic Development
Compensation: Per diem, in accordance with Section 112.061 of the Florida Statutes
Description: The committee has final approval authority in regard to which innovative investment projects are funded that have been submitted under this section.
Qualifications: The committee shall consist of 7 members, 1 appointed by the governor.

State Retirement Commission

Authority: Section 121.22, Florida Statutes
Term: 4 years
Confirmation Required: Senate
Oversight: Department of Management Services

Compensation: $100.00 per day for each day of service + per diem, in accordance with Section 112.061 of the Florida Statutes
Description: The commission hears appeals of retirees in regard to retirement problems that cannot be resolved by the Division of Retirement.
Qualifications: The commission shall consist of 3 members appointed by the governor. No person shall serve as a member who holds an elective office or serves as an agent for a political party. All members must have been citizens of Florida for at least 3 years prior to appointment.

Technology Research and Development Authority, Brevard County

Authority: Chapter 87-455, Laws of Florida
Term: 4 years
Confirmation Required: None
Oversight: County Jurisdiction
Compensation: Per diem, in accordance with Section 112.061 of the Florida Statutes
Description: The authority promotes scientific research and development and fosters higher education for the promotion of such research and development, in order to benefit the economic development of the county as a high technical/research center.
Qualifications: The Brevard County Legislative Delegation shall select 3 nominees for each vacancy. The governor shall appoint nominees to staggered terms.

Unemployment Appeals Commission

Authority: Section 20.171, Florida Statutes
Term: 4 years
Confirmation Required: Senate
Oversight: Agency for Workforce Innovation
Compensation: $100.00 per day service + per diem, in accordance with Section 112.061 of the Florida Statutes

Description: The commission is vested with all authority and responsibilities relating to unemployed compensation appeal proceedings. The commission may hold sessions and conduct hearings at any place within the State.

Qualifications: Three members shall be appointed by the governor. The chairperson shall have the qualifications required by law for a judge of the circuit court and shall not engage in any other business, vocation, or employment. The chairperson shall be compensated the same as a circuit court judge.

Workers' Compensation Panel

Authority: Section 440.13(12)(a) Florida Statutes
Term: Pleasure of the Governor
Confirmation Required: Senate
Oversight: Chief Financial Officer
Compensation: Per diem, in accordance with Section 112.061 of the Florida Statutes
Description: The panel determines fee schedules regarding reimbursement allowances for various treatments or services.
Qualifications: The panel shall consist of 3 members, 1 of whom shall be the insurance commissioner. The other 2 members shall be appointed by the governor.

Corrections / Courts / Juvenile Justice / Law Enforcement

The boards, commissions and senior level appointments listed in this chapter deal with issues that safeguard and protect the public. They help to provide a safe and humane environment for criminal offenders in Florida correctional facilities, and they work in partnership with the communities to provide programs and services for victims, victims' families, and offenders. They advise the governor on academic and vocational rehabilitation programs for offenders, on developing community alternatives to incarceration, and on the treatment of youthful offenders. Additionally, they advise the governor on matters of parole and sentencing, drug policy, and all aspects of solving drug-related problems in the state, including education, prevention, treatment, and law enforcement. To assist the state in carrying out its mandates to protect the public and ensure justice, the governor also appoints 3 capital collateral counselors, and a variety of special officers who are law enforcement personnel for private enterprises, but who are qualified by the state. Additionally, the governor appoints 18 different medical examiners who work in areas around the state.

Senior Level Appointment:

Secretary of the Department of Corrections
Secretary of the Department of Juvenile Justice
Executive Director of the Department of Law Enforcement
Director of the Office of Drug Control Policy
Chair of the Parole Commission
Capital Collateral Attorneys (3)
District Medical Examiners (18)

Boards and Commissions:

Battered Woman Syndrome Panels

Authority: Executive Order 92-80
Term: Pleasure of the Governor
Confirmation Required: None
Oversight: Parole Commission
Compensation: Per diem, in accordance with Section 112.061 of the Florida Statutes
Description: The panels review cases referred to them by the parole commission, to determine whether the clemency applicant had suffered from the Battered Woman Syndrome at the time of the commission of the crime for which he or she is incarcerated. The panels issue their final reports to the parole commission.
Qualifications: There shall be 3 special panels, each consisting of 3 members appointed by the governor and and the Cabinet. Each panel shall elect a chairperson.

Commission on the Administration of Justice in Capital Cases

Authority: Section 27.709, Florida Statutes
Term: 4 years
Confirmation Required: None
Oversight: State Legislature

Compensation: Per diem, in accordance with Section 112.061 of the Florida Statutes

Description: The commission reviews the administration of justice in capital collateral cases, receives relevant public input, reviews the operation of the capital collateral regional counsel, and advises and makes recommendations to the governor, the legislature, and state supreme court. The commission reviews complaints that have been filed with the Florida Bar, the state supreme court, or the Ethics Commission.

Qualifications: The governor, president of the senate, and the Speaker of the House, shall each appoint 2 members to the commission.

Correctional Privatization Commission

Authority: Section 957.03, Florida Statutes
Term: 4 years
Confirmation Required: None
Oversight: Department of Management Services
Compensation: Per diem, in accordance with Section 112.061 of the Florida Statutes

Description: The commission enters into a contract or contracts with one contractor per facility for the designing, acquiring, financing, leasing, constructing and operating of that facility. The commission must report to the Speaker of the House and the President of the Senate by December 1 each year on the status and effectiveness of the facilities under its management.

Qualifications: The commission consists of 5 members who are appointed by the governor, none of whom shall be an employee of the Department of Corrections. One member shall be a minority person, and 4 members shall be employed by the private sector.

Criminal and Juvenile Justice Information Systems Council

Authority: Section 943.06, Florida Statutes
Term: 4 years
Confirmation Required: None
Oversight: Department of Law Enforcement

Compensation: Per diem, in accordance with Section 112.061 of the Florida Statutes
Description: The council reviews operating policies and procedures and makes recommendations to the Department of Law Enforcement relating to criminal justice information.
Qualifications: No member of the legislature shall serve on the council. Five members shall be appointed by the governor.

Criminal and Juvenile Justice Standards and Training Commission

Authority: Section 943.11, Florida Statutes
Term: 4 years
Confirmation Required: None
Oversight: Department of Law Enforcement
Compensation: Per diem, in accordance with Section 112.061 of the Florida Statutes
Description: The commission has the power to set minimum standards for employment and the training of law enforcement and correctional officers. The commission also approves training institutions.
Qualifications: The governor shall appoint 15 of the 19 members on the commission. Except for correctional officers, only one member may be from an employing agency. Members may not be legislators, or serve in the following capacities while on the committee: secretary of the Department of Corrections, attorney general, commissioner of education, or the director of division of highway patrol.

Florida Corrections Commission

Authority: Section 20.315(4) Florida Statutes
Term: 4 years
Confirmation Required: Senate
Oversight: Department of Corrections
Compensation: Per diem, in accordance with Section 112.061 of the Florida Statutes

Description: The commission recommends major correctional policies for the governor's approval and assures that approved policies and any revisions thereto are properly executed. The commission periodically reviews the status of the state correctional system and recommends improvements therein to the governor and the legislature. It also provides public education on corrections and criminal justice issues.

Qualifications: The commission shall consist of 9 members appointed by the governor and subject to confirmation by the senate. The commission membership shall contain persons who are knowledgeable about construction, health care, information technology, education, business, food services, law, etc.

Florida Crime Laboratory Council

Authority: Section 943.355, Florida Statutes
Term: 4 years
Confirmation Required: None
Oversight: Department of Law Enforcement
Compensation: Per diem, in accordance with Section 112.061 of the Florida Statutes
Description: The council provides advice and makes recommendations to the executive director of the Florida Department of Law Enforcement to ensure proper fiscal accountability of State funding and effective operation of crime laboratories. The council also promotes the coordination of the criminal analysis laboratory system.
Qualifications: Two of the 10 members shall be appointed by the governor. Members appointed by the governor shall consist of a medical examiner and a circuit judge of a criminal court.

Florida Violent Crime and Drug Control Council

Authority: Section 943.031, Florida Statutes
Term: 2 years
Confirmation Required: None
Oversight: Department of Law Enforcement
Compensation: Per diem, in accordance with Section 112.061 of the Florida Statutes

Description: The Council provides advise and makes recommendations to the executive director on the following topics: the establishment of a program which provides grants to criminal justice agencies that develop and implement effective violent crime prevention and investigate programs; expansion of the use of an automated fingerprint identification system at the State and local level; the creation of a criminal justice research and behavioral science center.
Qualifications: The council shall consist of 14 members, 6 appointed by the governor. The governor must take into consideration representation by geography, population, ethnicity, and other relevant factors.

Juvenile Justice and Delinquency Prevention State Advisory Group

Authority: Executive Order 95-376
Term: Pleasure of the Governor
Confirmation Required: None
Oversight: Department of Juvenile Justice
Compensation: Per diem, in accordance with Section 112.061 of the Florida Statutes
Description: The advisory group operates as the supervisory board of the department for the purpose of supervising the preparation, implementation, and administration of the Juvenile Justice and Delinquency Prevention Plan. The department staff also carries out board policies related to the Juvenile Justice and Delinquency Prevention Plan.
Qualifications: The qualifications vary, according to district policies. The governor shall appoint chairperson. Members shall include, but are not limited to the following criteria:. the majority of the group shall not be full-time government employees. Whenever possible, 5 members shall represent ethnic minority groups.

Juvenile Welfare Board of Pinellas County

Authority: Chapter 00-427, Laws of Florida

Term: 4 years
Confirmation Required: Senate
Oversight: Judicial Branch
Compensation: Per diem, in accordance with Section 112.061 of the Florida Statutes
Description: The board provides and maintains juvenile guidance and guidelines in the county, psychological and psychiatric clinics for juveniles, care of dependent juveniles, the collection of data, and allocates funds to juvenile agencies.
Qualifications: The governor shall appoint 6 members. Other members of the board shall include the county superintendent of schools, a judge of the juvenile court, and the vice-chair of the board of county commissioners.

Medical Examiners Commission

Authority: Section 406.02, Florida Statutes
Term: 4 years
Confirmation Required: None
Oversight: Department of Law Enforcement
Compensation: Per diem, in accordance with Section 112.061 of the Florida Statutes
Description: The commission establishes medical examiner districts, oversees the distribution of state funds to the districts, and submits an annual report on the activities of district medical examiners.
Qualifications: Seven members shall be appointed by the governor. According to Section 406.02 of the Florida Statutes, members shall include the following: a state attorney, a public defender, a sheriff, a county commissioner, a funeral director, and 2 licensed physicians. Two additional members of the commission shall be the attorney general and the secretary of the Department of Health.

Parole Commission

Authority: Section 947.01, Florida Statutes
Term: 6 years
Confirmation Required: Senate and Cabinet

Oversight: Department of Corrections
Compensation: $85,355.00 per year + per diem, in accordance with Section 112.061 of the Florida Statutes
Description: The commission grants parole, performance investigations, and hearings for parole revocations, conducts investigations, and makes recommendations for executive clemency.
Qualifications: The parole commission shall consist of 3 members appointed by the governor and the cabinet for a term of 6 years. the parole qualification committee shall submit a list of 3 eligible applicants for each vacancy to the governor and cabinet.

Parole Qualifications Committee

Authority: Section 947.02, Florida Statutes
Term: 2 years
Confirmation Required: Cabinet
Oversight: County Jurisdiction
Compensation: Per diem, in accordance with Section 112.061 of the Florida Statutes
Description: The committee provides for statewide advertisement of vacancies on the commission; it also develops a plan for the determination of the qualification of applicaticants.
Qualifications: Members shall have special knowledge of penology, the administration of criminal justice, and offender rehabilitation programs.

Prison Rehabilitative Industries and Diversified Enterprises Board of Directors

Authority: Section 946.504, Florida Statutes
Term: 4 years
Confirmation Required: Senate
Oversight: Department of Corrections
Compensation: Per diem, in accordance with Section 112.061 of the Florida Statutes
Description: This is a non-profit corporation, which governs the state's prison industries and provides for a system of job training and placement of inmates. The corporation submits an annual report to the legislature.

Qualifications: There shall be 13 members on the board, all chosen by the governor. When a vacancy occurs the board of directors compiles a list of possible candidates. This board shall be non-profit and shall not require financial disclosure of any kind.

Sentencing Commission

Authority: Section 921.001, Florida Statutes
Term: 2 years
Confirmation Required: None
Oversight: Judicial Branch
Compensation: Per diem, in accordance with Section 112.061 of the Florida Statutes
Description: The sentencing commission is responsible for the development of a statewide system of sentencing guidelines.
Qualifications: The governor shall appoint 5 members with specific qualifications: the Chief Justice, the Speaker House of Representatives, president of the Senate, and the Attorney General. Designee may service on commission in place of the above. The president of the Senate also appoints one member..

State Council for Interstate Adult Offender Supervision

Authority: Section 949.072, Florida Statutes
Term: 4 years
Confirmation Required: None
Oversight: Department of Corrections
Compensation: Per diem, in accordance with Section 112.061 of the Florida Statutes
Description: The state council advises the compact administrator on participation in the interstate commission activities and the administration of the compact. Also, the council exercises oversight and advocacy concerning its participation in interstate commission activities and other duties, including the development of policy regarding operations and procedures of the compact within the state.

Qualifications: The state council shall consist of 7 members, 6 appointed by the governor. The secretary of corrections shall serve as the compact administrator for the state.

Victims Assistance Initiative, Inc.

Authority: Section 960.002, Florida Statutes
Term: 2 years
Confirmation Required: None
Oversight: Office of the governor
Compensation: Per diem, in accordance with Section 112.061 of the Florida Statutes
Description: The purposes of the corporation are exclusively charitable and educational within the meaning of the Internal Revenue Code, Section 501(c)(3). This not-for-profit corporation assists in addressing the needs of victims of adult and juvenile crimes, in accordance with Section 960.002, of the Florida Statutes. The board of directors manages the affairs of the corporation.
Qualifications: The board of directors shall consist of 9 members, appointed by the governor with terms ending in February. The number of directors may be increased or decreased but shall never be less than 3. Initial terms for members shall be staggered.

Judicial Appointments

The boards, commissions and senior level appointments listed in this chapter are charged with protecting the rights and liberties of Florida's citizens. They uphold and interpret the law, and provide for the peaceful resolution of disputes. As well, they advise the governor on the qualifications of potential appointees to the Florida judiciary system. Since judicial appointments are handled in a slightly different manner than other appointments through the use of judicial nominating commissions, a bit of background information is in order.

A brief overview of the court system is as follows: the highest court in Florida is the state supreme court, which has 7 justices. To be eligible to serve, a person must be a registered voter who resides in Florida; he or she must also have been admitted to the practice of law for the preceding 10 years by the state.

Next, 5 district courts of appeals, made up of 3-judge panels that review the merits of appealed trial court decisions. These judges must meet the same eligibility requirements as justices of the state supreme court. Like state supreme court justices, district court judges also serve terms of 6 years and are eligible for successive terms under a merit retention vote of the electors in their districts. These 5 districts are further subdivided into 20 circuit courts, which are made up of the 67 counties in the state.

Historically, Florida's judges were chosen by direct election. The only exception was when a vacancy occurred between elections. In that case, the governor appointed a replacement to serve until the next election could be held. However, the election process of judges led to many problems. Judges had to raise campaign money for their election; often the money was donated by the same attorneys who practiced before the court. The problem came to the public's attention in the mid-1970's, after several Florida appellate judges were charged with ethics violations. In 1971, Governor Reubin Askew took steps to reform the system by instituting a new system called "merit selection."

This system preserves the independence of the judiciary branch, and reduces political influences by not allowing the governor to directly select judges. Instead, the governor appoints judges from a list of candidates put forth by the judicial nominating commission. Under this system, an impartial panel suggests names of possible appointees to the governor; the governor then selects an individual whose application has been reviewed and which has been found qualified by the commission.

In 1974, Justice Ben F. Overton became the first state supreme court justice to have been chosen by this process; this system is still with us today.

Executive Level Appointments:

Judgeships:

Supreme Court

Courts of Appeal

Circuit Courts

County Courts

Judges of Compensation Claims

Boards and Commissions:

Appellate District Judicial Nominating Commissions (5):
First, Second, Third, Fourth and Fifth

Authority: Section 43.291, Florida Statutes
Term: 4 years
Confirmation Required: None
Oversight: Judicial Branch
Compensation: Per diem, in accordance with Section 112.061 of the Florida Statutes
Description: These commissions nominate 3 persons for the governor to consider, in filling a vacancy on a district court of appeals.
Qualifications: No judge shall be a member. Members may hold public office, but shall not be eligible for appointment to judicial office while on the committee and for 2 years thereafter. Members shall be residents of the territorial jurisdiction of the commission.

Judicial Nominating Commission, (20):
First through Twentieth Circuit

Authority: Section 43.291, Florida Statutes
Term: 4 years
Confirmation Required: None
Oversight: Judicial Branch
Compensation: Per diem, in accordance with Section 112.061 of the Florida Statutes
Description: The commission nominates 3 persons for the governor to consider in filling a vacancy on the Eighteenth Judicial Circuit Court.
Qualifications: No judge shall be a member. Members may hold public office, but shall not be eligible for appointment to judicial office while on the committee and for 2 years thereafter. Representation of each county shall be considered.

Judicial Qualifications Commissions

Authority: Section 43.20, Florida Statutes
Term: 6 years
Confirmation Required: None
Oversight: Judicial Branch
Compensation: Per diem, in accordance with Section 112.061 of the Florida Statutes
Description: The commission investigates and recommends to the state supreme court the reprimand or removal from office of any justice or judge whose conduct demonstrates an unfitness to hold office.
Qualifications: No member except a justice or judge shall be eligible for judicial office while on the commission and for 2 years thereafter. No member shall hold public office or an office in a political party while on the commission.

Statewide Nomination Commission

Authority: Section 440.45, Florida Statutes
Term: 4 years
Confirmation Required: None
Oversight: Judicial Branch
Compensation: Per diem, in accordance with Section 112.061 of the Florida Statutes
Description: The commission reviews the conduct of the judges of compensation claims and determines whether such judges should be retained in office. The commission submits to the governor 3 names for each vacancy.
Qualifications: The governor shall appoint 5 of the 15 members, and the board of governors of the Florida Bar shall appoint 5 members, also. These 10 appointed members shall appoint 5 additional members.

Supreme Court Judicial Nominating Commission

Authority: Section 43.291, Florida Statutes
Term: 4 years

Confirmation Required: None
Oversight: Judicial Branch
Compensation: Per diem, in accordance with Section 112.061 of the Florida Statutes
Description: The commission nominates 3 persons for the governor to consider in filling a vacancy on the state supreme court.
Qualifications: No judge shall be a member. Members may hold public office, but shall not be eligible for appointment to judicial office while on the committee and for 2 years thereafter.

THE FLORIDA GUIDE TO POLITICAL APPOINTMENTS

Education

The boards, commissions and senior level appointments listed in this chapter deal with education-related issues that increase the proficiency of all students and create an equitable and efficient educational system. They provide students of all ages with the opportunity to expand their knowledge and skills through learning, research, and parent and community partnerships, while employing an accountability system that measures student achievement and teacher recruitment and retention. They endeavor to create a skilled workforce via a coordinated, seamless, student-centered educational syste which has local operational flexibility.

In addition to the appointments mentioned in this chapter, the governor may fill vacancies due to resignation, death, removal, promotion, or other special circumstances (including appointments to locally elected school boards).

Senior Level Appointments:

Commissioner of Education

Chair of the State Board of Education

Chair of the Emerging Technology Commission

Chair of the Florida Board of Governors

Boards and Commissions:

Board of Control for Southern Regional Education

Authority: Section 244.02, Florida Statutes
Term: 4 years
Confirmation Required: None
Oversight: Department of Education
Compensation: Per diem, in accordance with Section 112.061 of the Florida Statutes
Description: The board plans for all phases of educational institutions in the regional compact which consists of: Alabama, Arkansas, Florida, Georgia, Kentucky, Louisiana, Maryland, Mississippi, North Carolina, South Carolina, Texas, Virginia, and West Virginia.
Qualifications: The governor shall serve as the ex-officio member and shall appoint 4 additional citizens, one from the field of education and one from the legislature.

Board of Directors, Florida Education Fund

Authority: Section 240.498, Florida Statutes
Term: 3 years
Confirmation Required: None
Oversight: Department of Education
Compensation: Per diem, in accordance with Section 112.061 of the Florida Statutes
Description: The board administers the Florida Endowment Fund for Higher Education, which is established to provide for programs which enhance the quality of higher educational opportunities in Florida.
Qualifications: The board shall consist of 12 members, 2 appointed by the governor, 2 by the president of the senate, and 2 by the Speaker of the House. Two members shall be appointed by the board of regents from the state university system, 2 by the state board of community colleges, and 2 by the state board of independent colleges.

Board of Directors, Florida Fund for Minority Teachers, Inc.

Authority: Section 240.4129, Florida Statutes
Term: 3 years
Confirmation Required: None
Oversight: University of Florida
Compensation: Per diem, in accordance with Section 112.061 of the Florida Statutes
Description: The Florida Fund for Minority Teachers, Inc., is created as a not-for-profit corporation. The corporation administers and manages the Florida Minority Teacher Education Scholars Program. The corporation submits an annual budget projection to the Department of Education to be included in the annual legislative budget request. The board appoints an executive director.
Qualifications: The governor shall appoint at least 15, but not more than, 25 members. At least 4 members must be employed by public community colleges, and at least 11 must be employed by public or private post-secondary institutes. The BOR, the state board of community colleges, and the state board of independent colleges and universities shall provide the governor with 15 recommendations.

Board of Trustees, Florida School for the Deaf and the Blind

Authority: Section 242.331, Florida Statutes
Term: 4 years
Confirmation Required: Senate
Oversight: Department of Education
Compensation: Per diem, in accordance with Section 112.061 of the Florida Statutes
Description: The board has complete jurisdiction over the management of the school and acts under the supervision and general policies of the state board of education.
Qualifications: Each member shall have been a resident of Florida for at least 10 years.

Board of Trustees, Florida Virtual High School

Authority: Section 228.082, Florida Statutes
Term: 4 years
Confirmation Required: None
Oversight: Department of Education
Compensation: Per diem, in accordance with Section 112.061 of the Florida Statutes
Description: The Florida On-Line School is established for the development and delivery of on-line and distance learning education. The board of trustees shall enter into agreements with distance learning providers.
Qualifications: The board of trustees shall consist of 7 members appointed by the governor. The governor shall designate the initial chairperson of the board of trustees.

Board of Trustees, Universities (11): Florida A and M, Florida Atlantic, Florida International, Florida State, Gulf Coast, New College of Florida, University of Central Florida, University of Florida, University of North Florida, University of South Florida, University of West Florida

Authority: Section 229.008, Florida Statutes
Term: 4 years
Confirmation Required: Senate
Oversight: Department of Education
Compensation: Per diem, in accordance with Section 112.061 of the Florida Statutes
Description: These boards are responsible for cost-effective policy decisions appropriate to the universities' missions, the implementation and maintenance of high-quality educational programs within the laws and rules of the state board of education, the measurement of performance, the reporting of information, and the provision of input regarding state policy, budgeting and educational standards.
Qualifications: The governor shall appoint members to the boards. In addition, each student body president shall serve as a

voting member. The governor shall consider diversity and regional representation, but there shall be no state residency requirement.

Charter School Review Panel

Authority: Section 228.056(20), Florida Statutes
Term: 1 years
Confirmation Required: None
Oversight: Department of Education
Compensation: Per diem, in accordance with Section 112.061 of the Florida Statutes
Description: The Charter School Review Panel reviews issues, practices, and policies regarding charter schools. The panel makes recommendations to the legislature, to the department of education, to charter schools, and to school districts for improving charter school operations and oversight. The panel also ensures best business practices and fair business relationships with charter schools.
Qualifications: The panel shall include 3 members appointed by the governor, and 2 appointees each from the commissioner of education, the president of the senate, and the Speaker of the House. Members shall have experience in finance, administration, law, education, and school governance.

College Reach-Out Advisory Council

Authority: Section 240.61, Florida Statutes
Term: 4 years
Confirmation Required: None
Oversight: Department of Education
Compensation: Per diem, in accordance with Section 112.061 of the Florida Statutes
Description: An advisory council reviews proposals and recommends to the state board of education an order of priority for funding the proposals.
Qualifications: The advisory council shall consist of 10 members, one appointed by the governor.

Commission for Independent Education

Authority: Section 229.0074, Florida Statutes
Term: 4 years
Confirmation Required: Senate
Oversight: Department of Education
Compensation: Per diem, in accordance with Section 112.061 of the Florida Statutes
Description: The commission oversees matters relating to independent postsecondary educational institutions, including consumer protection, program improvement, registration, authorization, licensure, and certification of exemption from licensure for institutions under its preview, in keeping with the state goals of the seamless K-20 educational system.
Qualifications: The commission shall consist of 6 members appointed by the governor.

Conversion Charter School Pilot Program Statewide Selection Panel

Authority: Section 228.0581, Florida Statutes
Term: 4 years
Confirmation Required: None
Oversight: Department of Education
Compensation: Per diem, in accordance with Section 112.061 of the Florida Statutes
Description: The panel reviews the conversion charter school pilot program applications submitted by the district school boards, and selects the 10 applications which the panel feels best comply with the purpose of the program. The purpose of the program is to produce significant improvements in student achievement and school management, and to encourage and measure the use of innovative learning methods.
Qualifications: The panel shall consist of 9 members, 3 appointed by the governor. The commissioner of education, the president of the senate, and the Speaker of the House shall each appoint 2 members.

Council for Education Policy, Research, and Improvement

Authority: Section 229.0031, Florida Statutes
Term: 6 years
Confirmation Required: None
Oversight: State Legislature
Compensation: Per diem, in accordance with Section 112.061 of the Florida Statutes
Description: The council conducts and reviews educational research, provides independent analysis of education progress, and provides independent evaluation of education issues of statewide concern.
Qualifications: The council shall consist of 9 members, 5 appointed by the governor. The senate president and Speaker of the House shall each appoint 2 members. Members shall not include elected officials or employees of public or independent educational entities.

District Board of Trustees, Community Colleges (28): Brevard, Broward, Central Florida, Chipola Junior College, Daytona Beach, Edison, Florida Community College at Jacksonville, Florida Keys, Gulf Coast, Hillsborough, Indian River, Lake-Sumter, Manatee, Miami-Dade, Okaloosa-Walton, North Florida, Palm Beach, Pasco-Hernando, Pensacola Junior College, Polk, Saint Johns River, Santa Fe, Seminole, South Florida, St. Petersburg Junior College, Lake City, Tallahassee, and Valencia Community College

Authority: Section 240.313, Florida Statutes
Term: 4 years
Confirmation Required: Senate and Cabinet
Oversight: Department of Education
Compensation: Per diem, in accordance with Section 112.061 of the Florida Statutes
Description: The board of trustees has the authority to adopt necessary rules for the proper operation of their respective community

college in accordance with or to supplement those rules prescribed by the state board of education.

Qualifications: There shall be 5 or 7 members representing each school board district, as the board so elects. There shall not be more than 9 members for 2 or more school districts. Procedures for approval of members shall be developed by the state board of education. Edison Community College shall have 9 board members; Lee County shall have 3 board members; Charlotte County ahall have 2 board members; Collier County shall 2 board members; Glades County and Hendry County shall have 1 board member each. South Florida Community College shall have 8 trustees; Highlands County shall have 4 trustees; Hardee County and DeSoto County shall have 2 trustees each.

Education Commission of the States

Authority: Section 244.06, .07, .08, Florida Statutes
Term: Pleasure of the Governor
Confirmation Required: None
Oversight: Federal Organization Titles
Compensation: Per diem, in accordance with Section 112.061 of the Florida Statutes
Description: A multi-state regional educational compact to establish and maintain close cooperation and understanding among executive, legislative, professional educators, and lay leadership on a nationwide basis.
Qualifications: Each member state is represented by 7 members. Florida membership shall be the governor, 2 members appointed by the governor, 2 members appointed by the president of the Senate, and 2 members appointed by the Speaker of the House.

Emerging Technology Commission

Authority: Section 240.72(3) Florida Statutes
Term: July 1, 2004
Confirmation Required: None
Oversight: Office of the governor

Compensation: Per diem, in accordance with Section 112.061 of the Florida Statutes

Description: The commission guides the establishment of centers of excellence. The purpose and objective of a center of excellence is to identify and pursue opportunities for university scholars, research center scientists and engineers, and private businesses to form collaborative partnerships. These partnerships foster and promote the research required to develop commercially advanced and innovative technologies.

Qualifications: The commission shall consist of 12 members, 5 appointed by the governor. The governor shall also appoint the chairperson. The regular members shall be business leaders, industrial researchers, academic researchers, scientists, or engineers in advanced technology sectors.

FCAT Blue Ribbon Task Force

Authority: Executive Order 02-108
Term: Pleasure of the Governor
Confirmation Required: None
Oversight: State Board of Education
Compensation: Per diem, in accordance with Section 112.061 of the Florida Statutes

Description: The task force makes recommendations regarding expanded accommodations for FCAT test-takers. The task force also considers the high school credentials and access to post-secondary education available to students with disabilities. As the time this book was published, the task force has completed its service and not active.

Qualifications: The task force shall be comprised of 11 members appointed by the governor. The chairperson shall also be appointed by the governor.

Florida Board of Governors

Authority: Article IX, Section 7 of the Florida Constitution
Term: 7 years
Confirmation Required: Senate

Oversight: Department of Education
Compensation: Per diem, in accordance with Section 112.061 of the Florida Statutes
Description: The board operates, controls, and is fully responsible for the management of the whole university system. The board's responsibilities include defining the distinctive mission of each constituent university and its articulation with free public schools and community colleges, ensuring the well planned coordination and operation of the system, and avoiding wasteful duplication of programs.
Qualifications: The board consists of 17 members, 14 appointed by the governor and subject to senate confirmation. The commissioner of education, the chair of the advisory council of faculty senates, and the president of The Florida Student Association shall also be members of the board.

Florida Endowment Foundation for Vocational Rehabilitation

Authority: Section 413.615, Florida Statutes
Term: 3 years
Confirmation Required: None
Oversight: Department of Education
Compensation: Per diem, in accordance with Section 112.061 of the Florida Statutes
Description: The Florida Endowment Foundation for Vocational Rehabilitation is created as a direct-support organization encouraging public and private support to enhance vocational rehabilitation and employment of citizens who are disabled.
Qualifications: The governor shall appoint 9 members to the board of directors for the foundation. They shall have an interest in service to persons with disabilities. Disabled individuals who meet the criteria shall be given special consideration for appointment.

Florida Independent Living Council, Inc.

Authority: Section 413.395, Florida Statutes

Term: 3 years
Confirmation Required: None
Oversight: Department of Education
Compensation: Per diem, in accordance with Section 112.061 of the Florida Statutes
Description: The Council jointly develops and submits, in conjunction with the division, The State Plan For Independent Living. The council monitors, reviews, and evaluates the implementation of the state plan for independent living. It coordinates activities with the Florida Rehabilitation Advisory Council and other councils to address the needs of specific disability populations and issues under other federal law.
Qualifications: The Council shall consist of a minimum of 14 members, excluding ex officio members. The members of the council shall be appointed by the governor after soliciting recommendations from the council.

Florida Martin Luther King, Jr. Institute for Non-violence

Authority: Section 240.631, Florida Statutes
Term: 5 years
Confirmation Required: None
Oversight: Miami Dade Community College
Compensation: Per diem, in accordance with Section 112.061 of the Florida Statutes
Description: The institute conducts training, provides symposia, and develops continuing education and programs to promote skills in non-violent conflict resolution for persons in government, private enterprise, community groups, and voluntary associations. The institute establishes fellowships through the awarding of financial assistance to individuals and organizations, enabling them to pursue scholarly inquiry and study strategies for peace.
Qualifications: The board shall consist of 13 members, 10 appointed by the governor. No more than 3 of the 6 regular members shall be of the same political party. No member shall serve on the board for more than 10 years.

Florida Prepaid College Board

Authority: Section 240.551(5), Florida Statutes
Term: 3 years
Confirmation Required: Senate
Oversight: Department of Insurance
Compensation: Per diem, in accordance with Section 112.061 of the Florida Statutes
Description: The board administers the Florida Prepaid Post-secondary Education Expense Program, which fosters timely financial planning for post-secondary education through advanced payment and investment.
Qualifications: See specific districts for guuidelines. The governor's appointees shall possess knowledge, skill, and experience in accounting, actuary, risk, or investment management. Any designees of other members must also satisfy the same requirements.

Florida Rehabilitation Council

Authority: Section 413.405, Florida Statutes
Term: 3 years
Confirmation Required: None
Oversight: Department of Education
Compensation: Per diem, in accordance with Section 112.061 of the Florida Statutes
Description: The council assists the division in the planning and development of statewide rehabilitation programs and services, and recommends improvement to such programs and services. The council also reviews, analyzes, and advises the division in regard to the performance of the responsibilities of the division under Title I.
Qualifications: The total council membership, excluding ex officio members, shall be 15 to 25 members. The governor shall appoint members, after soliciting recommendations from representatives of organizations representing a broad range of disabled individuals as well as organizations interested in those individuals.

Higher Education Facilities Financing Authority

Authority: Senate Bill 302
Term: 5 years
Confirmation Required: Senate
Oversight: Department of Education
Compensation: Per diem, in accordance with Section 112.061 of the Florida Statutes
Description: The commission establishes priorities for the identification, acquisition, protection, and preservation of historic and archaelogical sites and properties. The members serve as the legislative historic preservation advisory body, with respect to the collection and preservation of the historic records of both houses of the legislature.
Qualifications: The commission shall consist of 11 members, 7 of which are appointed by the governor in consultation with the secretary of state. The president of the Senate and the Speaker of the House shall each appoint 2 members. At least 1 member shall be a resident of a county with a population of 75,000 or less.

Land Acquisition and Facilities Advisory Board of Miami-Dade County School Board District

Authority: Chapter 01-253, Laws of Florida
Term: Pleasure of the Governor
Confirmation Required: None
Oversight: County Jurisdiction
Compensation: Per diem, in accordance with Section 112.061 of the Florida Statutes
Description: The advisory board provides expert advice and assists in improving the district's land acquisition and facilities operational processes. The board also makes all reasonable efforts to help the district correct deficiencies noted in the examination or audit of the district. The board shall assesses the district's progress and corrective actions and reports to the commissioner of education.

Qualifications: The advisory board consists of 7 members, 3 appointed by the governor. The president of the senate and the Speaker of the House shall each appoint 2 members. Members shall have the specific expertise needed to assist the school district in improving its deficiencies.

Learning Gateway Steering Committee

Authority: Senate Bill 1844
Term: 3 years
Confirmation Required: None
Oversight: Department of Education
Compensation: Per diem, in accordance with Section 112.061 of the Florida Statutes
Description: The purpose of the committee is to provide parents access to information, the referral process and services to lessen the effects of learning disabilities in children from birth to age 9. The committee provides policy development, consultation, oversight, and support for the implementation of 3 model programs. The committee also advises on statewide implementation of system components and issues.
Qualifications: The committee consists of 18 members. The governor, the president of the senate, and the Speaker of the House shall each appoint 6 members. The governor shall designate the chairperson of the committee.

Partnership for School Safety and Security

Authority: Section 229.8347, Florida Statutes
Term: 4 years
Confirmation Required: Senate
Oversight: Department of Education
Compensation: Per diem, in accordance with Section 112.061 of the Florida Statutes
Description: The partnership evaluates school safety, security programs, and strategies based on controlled scientific research. It also recommends information to be included in the electronic

clearinghouse of safety and security information, makes recommendations for inclusion in the clearinghouse of safety and security information, and makes recommendations to the legislature for funding school safety and security programs.
Qualifications: The partnership shall consist of 11 members appointed by the governor and confirmed by the Senate. Three members shall be consumers who are not, and have never been, providers of school safety or security services. A vacancy shall be declared if 3 consecutive meetings are missed.

State Apprenticeship Advisory Council

Authority: Section 446.045, Florida Statutes
Term: 4 years
Confirmation Required: None
Oversight: Department of Education
Compensation: Per diem, in accordance with Section 112.061 of the Florida Statutes
Description: The council is advisory to the division of labor of the Florida Department of Labor and Employment Security on matters governing the terms and conditions of the apprentice's employment and training.
Qualifications: Ten members shall be appointed by the governor. These members shall represent industries having registered apprenticeship programs, or in which a need for apprenticeship programs has been demonstrated.

State Board of Education

Authority: Section 229.004, Florida Statutes
Term: 4 years
Confirmation Required: Senate
Oversight: State Board of Education
Compensation: Per diem, in accordance with Section 112.061 of the Florida Statutes
Description: The board serves as the corporate body for Florida's seamless K-12 educational system, implements the coor-

dinated educational vision, and oversees the success of that vision. The board enforces all laws, rules, and guidelines, and provides timely direction, resources, assistance, intervention when needed, as well as strong incentives and penalties to force accountability for results.

Qualifications: The board shall consist of 7 members. Members shall be residents of the state appointed by the governor. Members may be reappointed for additional terms, which shall not exceed 8 years of consecutive service. The governor shall appoint the first chairperson of the board.

Health / Health Care Administration / Elder Affairs

The boards, commissions and senior level appointments listed in this chapter work with issues that promote and protect the health and safety of Florida residents. This is accomplished by caring for the health of mothers and children, tracking diseases, maintaining healthy environments, promoting healthy lifestyles, providing services directly to residents and communities in need, and operating clinics that deliver health services. Healthcare-related appointments include advisory boards that cover issues ranging from biomedical research to substance abuse, and quality assurance boards, which oversee medical, dental, and clinical laboratories, as well as nursing home professionals. They may advise the governor on all health matters, including health care financing, planning, purchasing and regulatory functions; health facility licensure, regulation, inspection, and construction; health policy; hospital budget review; and the Medicaid Program. Other areas of concern include review of long-term care services, assisted living facilities training, adult day care food programs, and senior community service employment.

In addition to the appointments mentioned in this chapter, the governor may fill vacancies due to resignation, death, removal, promotion or other special circumstances, including appointments to: local hospital boards and authorities, healthcare districts and regional long-term care ombudsman councils.

Senior Level Appointments:

Secretary of the Department of Health
Secretary of the Agency for Health Care Administration
Secretary of the Department of Elder Affairs
Director of the Office of Long Term Care Policy

Boards and Commissions:

Alzheimer's Disease Advisory Committee

Authority: Section 430.501, Florida Statutes
Term: 4 years
Confirmation Required: None
Oversight: Department of Elderly Affairs
Compensation: Per diem, in accordance with Section 112.061 of the Florida Statutes
Description: The committee advises the department regarding legislative, programmatic and administrative matters that relate to Alzheimer's disease victims and their caretakers.
Qualifications: Members of the committee shall include Florida residents, who are experts in Alzheimer's disease. At least 4 to 10 members shall be licensed pursuant to Chapter 458–459 Florida Statutes or hold a Ph.D. degree and shall be currently involved in the research of Alzheimer's Disease.

Annual Report on Graduate Medical Education Committee

Authority: Chapter 01-222, Laws of Florida
Term: 4 years
Confirmation Required: None
Oversight: Department of Health
Compensation: Per diem, in accordance with Section 112.061 of the Florida Statutes

Description: The committee produces an annual report on graduate medical education, which includes the role of residents and medical faculty in the provision of health care, the cost of training medical residents for hospitals, medical schools, and teaching hospitals (including all hospital-medical affiliations), and the development of practice plans at all of the medical schools and municipalities.

Qualifications: The committee shall consist of 11 members, 2 of which shall be appointed by the governor.

Baker County Hospital Authority

Authority: Chapter 92-265, Laws of Florida
Term: 4 years
Confirmation Required: None
Oversight: County Jurisdiction
Compensation: Per diem, in accordance with Section 112.061 of the Florida Statutes
Description: The authority maintains a public hospital, employs and discharges all persons who may be employed by the hospital, and also has charge over all public monies appropriated to the authority.
Qualifications: Each member of the authority shall be a citizen and resident of Baker County. No person shall be a member who is engaged in the practice of medicine, interested directly or indirectly in any drug business, or who serves in local or state government positions.

Biomedical Research Advisory Council

Authority: Section 215.5602, Florida Statutes
Term: 3 years
Confirmation Required: None
Oversight: Department of Health
Compensation: Per diem, in accordance with Section 112.061 of the Florida Statutes
Description: The council addresses the health care problems of Floridians in the following areas: cancer, cardiovascular disease,

stroke, and pulmonary disease. The council develops criteria and standards for the award of research grants. It also advises the secretary of health as to the direction and scope of the biomedical research program.
Qualifications: The council shall consist of 9 members. The governor shall appoint 6 Floridians with biomedical and lay expertise in the general areas of cancer, cardiovascular disease, stroke, and pulmonary disease. Members shall not serve more than 2 consecutive terms.

Board of Acupuncture

Authority: Section 457.103, Florida Statutes
Term: 4 years
Confirmation Required: Senate
Oversight: Department of Health
Compensation: Per diem, in accordance with Section 112.061 of the Florida Statutes
Description: The board makes all rules concerning the licensing of acupuncturists in the state and regulates their activities to protect the health and safety of Floridians.
Qualifications: Members shall be appointed for a 4 year term or for the remainder of the unexpired term of a vacancy.

Board of Athletic Training

Authority: Section 468.703, Florida Statutes
Term: 4 years
Confirmation Required: Senate
Oversight: Department of Health
Compensation: Per diem, in accordance with Section 112.061 of the Florida Statutes
Description: The board is authorized to adopt rules which include, but are not limited to, the allowable scope of practice regarding the use of equipment, procedures, and medication requirements for a written protocol between the athletic trainer and a supervising physician, licensure requirements, licensure

examination, continuing education requirements, fees, and any other requirements necessary to regulate the practice of athletic training.

Qualifications: The board shall consist of 9 members who shall be appointed by the governor and confirmed by the senate.

Board of Chiropractic Medicine

Authority: Section 460.404, Florida Statutes

Term: 4 years

Confirmation Required: Senate

Oversight: Department of Health

Compensation: Per diem, in accordance with Section 112.061 of the Florida Statutes

Description: The board is authorized to set licensing fees and educational standards for certification as a chiropractic physician or physician's assistant The board also establishes guidelines for disciplinary cases.

Qualifications: Members shall be residents of Florida. Pursuant to Chapters 87-172 of the laws of Florida, at least 1 member shall be 60 years of age or older.

Board of Clinical Laboratory Personnel

Authority: Section 483.805, Florida Statutes

Term: 4 years

Confirmation Required: Senate

Oversight: Department of Health

Compensation: Per diem, in accordance with Section 112.061 of the Florida Statutes

Description: The board is authorized to adopt such rules, not inconsistent with law, as may be necessary to carry out the duties and authority conferred upon the board. The board, by rule, establishes fees to be paid for the application, examination, re-examination, licensing and renewal, reinstatement, and record-making and record keeping of health professionals.

Qualifications: The board shall consist of 7 members who shall be appointed by the governor and confirmed by the senate. Terms shall be for 4 years, expiring on October 31. A member may serve the remaining portion of an unexpired term, in addition to 2 consecutive 4 year terms.

Board of Clinical Social Work, Marriage and Family Therapy, and Mental Health Counseling

Authority: Section 491.004, Florida Statutes
Term: 4 years
Confirmation Required: Senate
Oversight: Department of Health
Compensation: Per diem, in accordance with Section 112.061 of the Florida Statutes
Description: The board adopts rules to govern the licensure of clinical social workers, marriage and family therapists, and mental health counselors. The definitions of the above are established by rule of the board.
Qualifications: The governor shall appoint 9 members to the board for staggered terms. Members shall include the following: 2 licensed social workers, 2 marriage and family therapists, and 2 mental health counselors. The other 3 members shall be citizens of Florida not connected to the profession.

Board of Commissioners, Halifax Hospital Medical Center

Authority: Chapter 84-539, Laws of Florida
Term: 4 years
Confirmation Required: None
Oversight: County Jurisdiction
Compensation: Per diem, in accordance with Section 112.061 of the Florida Statutes
Description: The district may establish and maintain such hospitals, medical facilities, clinics, and outpatient facilities and services as are necessary.
Qualifications: Members shall be residents of the district and shall post bond before assuming office.

Board of Commissioners, North Broward Hospital District

Authority: Chapter 63-1192, Laws of Florida
Term: 4 years
Confirmation Required: None
Oversight: County Jurisdiction
Compensation: Per diem, in accordance with Section 112.061 of the Florida Statutes
Description: Board members establish, construct, operate and maintain a hospital or hospitals, as is necessary to protect the health of the residents of the area.
Qualifications: One commissioner shall be a member of the medical profession. Each sub-district shall have 1 member. Members shall post bond before assuming office.

Board of Commissioners, South Broward Hospital District

Authority: Chapter 69-910, Laws of Florida
Term: 4 years
Confirmation Required: None
Oversight: County Jurisdiction
Compensation: Per diem, in accordance with Section 112.061 of the Florida Statutes
Description: The board may issue bonds for the purpose of raising funds to establish, construct, and maintain a hospital or hospitals, as is necessary to protect the health of the residents of the district.
Qualifications: Commissioners shall not be in the medical profession. They shall be qualified electors and property owners who have resided in Broward County for at least 1 year and in the sub-district for 90 days.

Board of Dentistry

Authority: Section 466.004, Florida Statutes
Term: 4 years
Confirmation Required: Senate
Oversight: Department of Health

Compensation: Per diem, in accordance with Section 112.061 of the Florida Statutes

Description: The board sets licensing and examination fees, determines competencies for testing, and certifies all qualified applicants for licensure as dentists and dental hygienists.

Qualifications: Dental members shall be licensed dentists who are actively engaged in the practice of dentistry in this state and have been engaged in their profession for at least 5 years preceding appointment. Pursuant to Chapter 87-172 of the laws of Florida, at least 1 member shall be 60 years of age or older.

Board of Directors, Florida Alzheimer's Center and Research Institute

Authority: Senate Bill 46-E
Term: 3 years
Confirmation Required: None
Oversight: University of South Florida
Compensation: Per diem, in accordance with Section 112.061 of the Florida Statutes

Description: The board of directors receives, holds, invests, and administers property and any monies acquired from private, local, state, and federal sources; this includes technical and professional income generated or derived from practice activities of the institute for the benefit of the institute, and the fulfillment of its mission.

Qualifications: The board shall consist of 16 to 21 members. For the initial appointments, the governor shall appoint 4 members; the president of the senate and the Speaker of the House shall each appoint 5 members. Upon expiration of initial terms, the board shall make appointments to fill vacancies.

Board of Directors, Florida Center for Nursing

Authority: Section 464.0196, Florida Statutes
Term: 3 years
Confirmation Required: None
Oversight: Department of Health

Compensation: Per diem, in accordance with Section 112.061 of the Florida Statutes
Description: The board addresses issues of supply and demand for nursing, including issues of recruitment, retention, and utilization of nurse work force resources.
Qualifications: The board shall consist of 16 members appointed by the governor. Recommendations shall come from the senate president, the Speaker of the House and the Florida State Board of Education. A simple majority of the board must be nurses of various practice areas. Members shall serve only 2 consecutive terms.

Board of Hearing Aid Specialists

Authority: Section 484.042, Florida Statutes
Term: 4 years
Confirmation Required: Senate
Oversight: Department of Health
Compensation: Per diem, in accordance with Section 112.061 of the Florida Statutes
Description: The board regulates the dispensing of hearing aids in the state and conducts and interprets hearing tests for selecting hearing aids. The board also conducts tests for hearing aids specialists.
Qualifications: The board shall consist of 9 members who are appointed by the governor and subject to senate confirmation. Five members shall be hearing aid specialists, and 4 members shall be lay members.

Board of Massage Therapy

Authority: Section 480.035, Florida Statutes
Term: 4 years
Confirmation Required: Senate
Oversight: Department of Health
Compensation: Per diem, in accordance with Section 112.061 of the Florida Statutes
Description: The board adopts rules for licensure, establishes minimum training programs for apprentices, specifies areas of

competency to be examined, governs the operation of massage establishments and sets fees.
Qualifications: Board members shall include a high school graduate and a citizen of the United States with residency in Florida for 5 years. They shall take the constitutional oath of office and shall not serve more than 2 terms.

Board of Medicine

Authority: Section 458.307, Florida Statutes
Term: 4 years
Confirmation Required: Senate
Oversight: Department of Health
Compensation: Per diem, in accordance with Section 112.061 of the Florida Statutes
Description: The board certifies applicants as physicians and physician assistants, establishes regulations for licensure, imposes penalties for violation of the act, and adopts standards for physician assistants.
Qualifications: Members shall be residents of Florida. Pursuant to Chapter 87-172 of the laws of Florida, professional members shall have practiced medicine for 4 years; shall not be connected with a medical college so that it provides principal income; and at least 1 member shall be 60 years of age or older.

Board of Nursing

Authority: Section 464.004, Florida Statutes amended
Term: 4 years
Confirmation Required: Senate
Oversight: Department of Health
Compensation: Per diem, in accordance with Section 112.061 of the Florida Statutes
Description: The board adopts licensing fees and requirements, provides rules under the Nurse Practice Act, and prescribes educational objectives, faculty qualifications, curriculum guidelines and procedures.

Qualifications: All members shall be residents of Florida. All professional members shall have been engaged in their profession for 4 years and should represent diverse areas of practice. Pursuant to Chapter 87-172 of the laws of Florida, at least 1 member shall be 60 years of age or older.

Board of Nursing Home Administrators

Authority: Section 468.1665, Florida Statutes
Term: 4 years
Confirmation Required: Senate
Oversight: Department of Health
Compensation: Per diem, in accordance with Section 112.061 of the Florida Statutes
Description: The board develops standards for licensure of nursing home administrators and ensures that those standards are met; licenses qualified applicants, and takes action on disciplinary cases.
Qualifications: Only board members who are nursing home administrators may have a direct financial interest in any nursing home. Pursuant to Chapter 87-172 of the laws of Florida, at least 1 member shall be 60 years of age or older.

Board of Occupational Therapy Practice

Authority: Section 468.205, Florida Statutes
Term: 4 years
Confirmation Required: Senate
Oversight: Department of Health
Compensation: Per diem, in accordance with Section 112.061 of the Florida Statutes
Description: The board is authorized to adopt such rules, not inconsistent with law, as may be necessary to carry out the duties and authority conferred upon the board to protect the health, safety, and welfare of the public.
Qualifications: The board shall consist of 7 members who are appointed by the governor and subject to senate confirmation. all members shall be residents of the state.

Board of Opticianry

Authority: Section 484.003, Florida Statutes
Term: 4 years
Confirmation Required: Senate
Oversight: Department of Health
Compensation: Per diem, in accordance with Section 112.061 of the Florida Statutes
Description: The board makes rules relating to standards of practice, minimum equipment which shall be used, procedures for transfer of prescription files, and penalties for violation of statutory provisions.
Qualifications: Five members shall be licensed opticians, and 2 members shall be lay persons. All members shall be residents of the state. Pursuant to Chapter 87-172 of the laws of Florida, at least 1 member shall be 60 years of age or older.

Board of Optometry

Authority: Section 463.003, Florida Statutes
Term: 4 years
Confirmation Required: Senate
Oversight: Department of Health
Compensation: Per diem, in accordance with Section 112.061 of the Florida Statutes
Description: The board sets licensing fees and requirements and adopts rules for standards of practice, including equipment to be used, prescription file procedures, and the handling of patients' medical records.
Qualifications: Five members shall be licensed optometrists in good standing, and 2 members shall be citizens who are not connected with the practice of optometry. Pursuant to Chapter 87-172 of the laws of Florida, at least 1 member shall be 60 years of age or older.

Board of Orthotics, Prosthetics, and Pedorthics

Authority: Section 468.801, Florida Statutes
Term: 4 years

Confirmation Required: Senate
Oversight: Department of Health
Compensation: Per diem, in accordance with Section 112.061 of the Florida Statutes
Description: The board adopts rules relating to standards of practice for orthotists, prosthetists, and pedorthists. The board adopts rules establishing a procedure for the biennial license renewal. The board also establishes a procedure for approving continuing education courses and may set a fee for the courses.
Qualifications: The board shall consist of 7 members who are appointed by the governor and confirmed by the senate. Members shall be residents of the state.

Board of Osteopathic Medicine

Authority: Section 459.004, Florida Statutes
Term: 4 years
Confirmation Required: Senate
Oversight: Department of Health
Compensation: Per diem, in accordance with Section 112.061 of the Florida Statutes
Description: The board certifies qualified applicants, imposes penalties for violation of statutory regulations, adopts standards for the training of osteopathic physician's assistants, and sets licensing fees.
Qualifications: Members shall be citizens of Florida. Pursuant to Chapter 87-172 of the laws of Florida, at least 1 member shall be 60 years of age or older.

Board of Pharmacy

Authority: Section 465.004, Florida Statutes
Term: 4 years
Confirmation Required: Senate
Oversight: Department of Health
Compensation: Per diem, in accordance with Section 112.061 of the Florida Statutes

Description: The board certifies qualified applicants, prescribes continuing education requirements, imposes penalties for violations of statutory regulations, and adopts rules for the public health and safety.
Qualifications: Members shall be residents of Florida. No person shall be appointed as a lay member who is in any way connected with a drug manufacturer or wholesaler. Pursuant to Chapter 87-172 of the laws of Florida, at least 1 member shall be 60 years of age or older.

Board of Physical Therapy Practice

Authority: Section 486.023, Florida Statutes
Term: 4 years
Confirmation Required: Senate
Oversight: Department of Health
Compensation: Per diem, in accordance with Section 112.061 of the Florida Statutes
Description: The board may administer oaths, summon witnesses, and take testimony in all matters relating to its duties under this chapter. It also establishes or modifies minimum standards of practice, and adopts or amends rules necessary to administer this chapter.
Qualifications: The governor shall appoint 7 members who shall be subject to confirmation by the senate. Five members shall be licensed physical therapists and 2 shall be lay members.

Board of Podiatric Medicine

Authority: Section 461.004, Florida Statutes
Term: 4 years
Confirmation Required: Senate
Oversight: Department of Health
Compensation: Per diem, in accordance with Section 112.061 of the Florida Statutes
Description: The board certifies qualified applicants, prescribes continuing education requirements, sets guidelines for the disposition of disciplinary cases, and develops podiatric residency programs in Florida hospitals.

Qualifications: Members shall be residents of Florida. Pursuant to Chapter 87-172 of the laws of Florida, at least 1 member shall be 60 years of age or older.

Board of Psychology

Authority: Section 490.004, Florida Statutes
Term: 4 years
Confirmation Required: Senate
Oversight: Department of Health
Compensation: Per diem, in accordance with Section 112.061 of the Florida Statutes
Description: The board certifies qualified applicants as psychologists, issues penalties for disciplinary cases, and ensures that provisions of the Psychological Services Act are met.
Qualifications: Five members shall be licensed psychologists, and 2 shall be lay members. Members shall serve 4 year terms. Pursuant to Chapter 87-172 of the laws of Florida, at least 1 member shall be 60 years of age or older.

Board of Respiratory Care

Authority: Section 468.354, Florida Statutes
Term: 4 years
Confirmation Required: Senate
Oversight: Department of Health
Compensation: Per diem, in accordance with Section 112.061 of the Florida Statutes
Description: The board establishes minimum standards for the delivery of respiratory care services. The board may adopt rules for this purpose, including rules governing the investigation, inspection, and review of schools and colleges that offer courses in respiratory care, in order to ascertain their compliance with standards established by the board or appropriate accrediting agencies.
Qualifications: The board shall be composed of 7 members appointed by the governor and confirmed by the Senate. No member shall serve more than 2 consecutive terms.

Board of Speech-Language Pathology and Audiology

Authority: Section 468.1135, Florida Statutes
Term: 4 years
Confirmation Required: Senate
Oversight: Department of Health
Compensation: Per diem, in accordance with Section 112.061 of the Florida Statutes
Description: The board, by rule, establishes fees to be paid for the application, examination, reexamination, licensing and renewal, reinstatement, and record-making and record-keeping.
Qualifications: The governor shall appoint 7 members to the board, subject to senate confirmation. Pursuant to Chapter 87-172 of the laws of Florida, at least 1 member shall be 60 years of age or older. Each speech-language pathologist and audiologist shall hold a valid certificate and be engaged in the practice for not less than 3 years prior to being appointed.

Campbellton-Graceville Hospital Corporation

Authority: Chapter 61-2290, Laws of Florida
Term: 4 years
Confirmation Required: None
Oversight: County Jurisdiction
Compensation: Per diem, in accordance with Section 112.061 of the Florida Statutes
Description: Members maintain a county hospital and may appoint a suitable hospital superintendent and other employees.
Qualifications: The governor shall appoint members from the community at large, with reference to their fitness for office.

Cape Canaveral Hospital District, Brevard County

Authority: Chapter 59-1129, Laws of Florida
Term: 4 years
Confirmation Required: None
Oversight: County Jurisdiction
Compensation: Per diem, in accordance with Section 112.061 of the Florida Statutes

Description: The board maintains a hospital and any other health-related structures, adopts all rules and regulations necessary for the efficient operation of the hospital, and employs non-medical personnel.

Qualifications: Members shall be qualified electors and property owners residing within the district.

Community Hospital Educational Council

Authority: Section 381.040, Florida Statutes
Term: 4 years
Confirmation Required: None
Oversight: Department of Health
Compensation: Per diem, in accordance with Section 112.061 of the Florida Statutes
Description: The council advises the Department of Health on statewide medical education. Medical institutions may apply to the council for grants-in-aid to support their approved programs
Qualifications: Eleven members shall be appointed by the governor. Seven members shall be a program director or a practicing physician in various fields (family practice, internal medicine, pediatrics, ob-gyn, emergency services, or psychiatry, with at least 1 licensed pursuant to Chapter 459). The other 4 members shall include: a dean of state medical school, a hospital administrator, and 2 consumer or lay members.

Continuing Care Advisory Council

Authority: Section 651.121, Florida Statutes
Term: 3 years
Confirmation Required: None
Oversight: Department of Insurance
Compensation: Per diem, in accordance with Section 112.061 of the Florida Statutes
Description: The board acts in an advisory capacity to the Department of Insurance, recommends needed changes in rules, and assists in the rehabilitation of continuing care operations.

Qualifications: Board members shall be a Florida resident in addition to geographically representing the state. See specific districts for qualification guidelines.

Department of Elderly Affairs Advisory Council

Authority: Section 430.05, Florida Statutes
Term: 3 years
Confirmation Required: None
Oversight: Department of Elderly Affairs
Compensation: Per diem, in accordance with Section 112.061 of the Florida Statutes
Description: The council serves in an advisory capacity to the secretary of elderly affairs, assisting in carrying out the purposes, duties, and responsibilities of the department. The council may make recommendations to the secretary, governor, Speaker, and senate president, regarding organizational issues and additions or reductions in the department's duties and responsibilities.
Qualifications: Each planning and service area of the agency on aging shall nominate 3 persons (1 of whom shall be 60 years of age or older), and the governor shall appoint 1 of these persons to the board. The governor shall also appoint 2 additional members. A majority of the members shall be 60 years of age or older.

Diabetes Advisory Council

Authority: Section 385.203, Florida Statutes
Term: 4 years
Confirmation Required: None
Oversight: Department of Health
Compensation: Per diem, in accordance with Section 112.061 of the Florida Statutes
Description: The council advises and consults with deans of medical schools and the secretary of department of health in developing overall policy and procedures to establish a statewide health care delivery system for diabetes.

Qualifications: The governor shall appoint 25 members, with advise from the secretary of health. Members shall be appointed for 4 year terms. The council shall elect a chairperson.

Florida Cancer Control and Research Advisory Council

Authority: Section 240.5121 (4), Florida Statutes
Term: 4 Years
Confirmation Required: None
Oversight: Department of Health
Compensation: Per diem, in accordance with Section 112.061 of the Florida Statutes
Description: The board advises the secretary of human resource services and approves a program each year for cancer control and research. The board also recommends a plan for the care and treatment of persons suffering from cancer.
Qualifications: The governor shall appoint 33 to 35 members, who shall be Florida residents. The senate president and the House Speaker shall each appoint 1 member. Pursuant to Chapter 87-172 of the laws of Florida, at least 1 member shall be 60 years of age or older. A minimum of 10 members shall be minority persons as defined by Statute 288.703(3). The governor shall appoint the chairperson.

Florida Developmental Disabilities Council

Authority: Federal Law 101-496
Term: 4 years
Confirmation Required: None
Oversight: Department of Health
Compensation: Per diem, in accordance with Section 112.061 of the Florida Statutes
Description: The council serves as an advocate for persons with developmental disabilities, and reviews and comments on all state plans affecting the developmentally disabled.
Qualifications: Members shall be Florida residents. At least half of the members shall be consumers, developmentally disabled, or parents or guardians of a developmentally disabled person.

Florida Employee Long-Term Care Plan Board of Directors

Authority: Chapter 98-400, Laws of Florida
Term: 2 years
Confirmation Required: None
Oversight: Department of Elderly Affairs
Compensation: Per diem, in accordance with Section 112.061 of the Florida Statutes
Description: The board prepares an annual report of the plan with the assistance of an actuarial consultant, approves the appointment of an executive director jointly recommended by the division and the department to serve as the chief administrative and operational officer of the board, and implements other policies and procedures as necessary to assure the soundness and efficient operation of the plan.
Qualifications: The board shall be composed of 7 members, 3 appointed by the governor.

Florida Health Access Corporation

Authority: Section 408.0014, Florida Statutes
Term: 3 years
Confirmation Required: None
Oversight: Department of Health
Compensation: Per diem, in accordance with Section 112.061 of the Florida Statutes
Description: The corporation establishes and administers a program for the division of group health insurance to small businesses through the pooling of employees into larger groups. The Florida Health Access Corporation shall contract for insurance as a non-profit corporation.
Qualifications: Seven members shall be appointed by the governor. The appointed members shall include: 3 who represent small business; 3 from the health care administration field; and 1 lay member.

Florida Interagency Coordinating Council for Infants and Toddlers

Authority: 34 Codes of Federal Regulation, Section 303.600

Term: 3 years

Confirmation Required: None

Oversight: Department of Health

Compensation: Per diem, in accordance with Section 112.061 of the Florida Statutes

Description: The Council is established to enhance opportunities for Florida's infants and toddlers with special needs and their families. The Council advises and assists the state lead agency and other entities in the development, implementation, and evaluation of policies and procedures, and educates decision-makers, service providers, families, and other Floridians who may benefit from their services.

Qualifications: The council shall be appointed by the governor. The governor shall ensure that the membership of the council reasonably represents the population of the State.

Governor's Panel on Excellence in Long-Term Care

Authority: Section 400.235(3), Florida Statutes

Term: 4 years

Confirmation Required: None

Oversight: Office of the governor

Compensation: Per diem, in accordance with Section 112.061 of the Florida Statutes

Description: The panel develops and implements an award and recognition program, known as the Gold Seal Program, for nursing facilities that demonstrate excellence in long-term care over a sustained period. The panel reviews nominees and makes a recommendation to the governor for final approval and award.

Qualifications: The panel shall consist of 12 members, 3 appointed by the governor. No member shall serve for more than 2 consecutive 4 year terms. Members are prohibited from having any ownership interest in a nursing facility.

Hamilton County Memorial Hospital Board

Authority: Section 155.06, Florida Statutes
Term: 4 years
Confirmation Required: None
Oversight: County Jurisdiction
Compensation: Per diem, in accordance with Section 112.061 of the Florida Statutes
Description: The board adopts such bylaws, as may be necessary, for their own guidance and for the government of the hospital. They shall have exclusive control of the expenditures.
Qualifications: Members shall be considered members-at-large and shall take an oath of office.

Hardee County Indigent Health Care Special District

Authority: County Ordinance 93-03
Term: 4 years
Confirmation Required: None
Oversight: County Jurisdiction
Compensation: Per diem, in accordance with Section 112.061 of the Florida Statutes
Description: The district board provides for the health care of qualified indigent patients residing in Hardee County through the purchase or reimbursement of inpatient, outpatient, and emergency medical services for said indigent patients. The district collects information and statistical data that will be helpful to the board and the county in deciding the health care needs in the county.
Qualifications: The board shall consist of 5 members, 2 appointed by the governor and 3 by the board of county commissioners. Members shall have been residents of the Hardee County for the past 12 months. No member shall serve for more than 2 consecutive terms. Vacancies shall be filled by the county commission for unexpired terms.

Health Care District of Palm Beach County

Authority: Chapter 92-340, Laws of Florida
Term: 4 years

Confirmation Required: None
Oversight: County Jurisdiction
Compensation: Per diem, in accordance with Section 112.061 of the Florida Statutes
Description: The district board of the Palm Beach County Health Care District is vested with the authority and responsibility to provide for the comprehensive planning and delivery of adequate health care facilities and services for the citizens of Palm Beach County, particularly medically needy citizens. (This includes, but not limited to, hospitals.)
Qualifications: The board shall consist of 7 members, 3 appointed by the governor. At least 1 member shall reside in the geographic area represented by each subdistrict. Terms shall be for 4 years ending September 30. No member of the board shall serve more than 2 consecutive terms.

Health Information Systems Council

Authority: Section 381.90, Florida Statutes
Term: 2 years
Confirmation Required: None
Oversight: Department of Health
Compensation: Per diem, in accordance with Section 112.061 of the Florida Statutes
Description: The Council is created to facilitate the identification, collection, standardization, sharing, and coordination of health related data, including fraud and abuse data. The council also facilitates professional and facility licensing data among federal, state, local, and private entities.
Qualifications: The governor shall appoint 2 of the 10 council members. Terms of office for members appointed by the governor shall begin January 1 and end December 31. Representatives of the federal government may serve without voting rights.

Hospital Board of DeSoto County

Authority: Chapter 65-1450, Laws of Florida

Term: 4 years
Confirmation Required: None
Oversight: County Jurisdiction
Compensation: Per diem, in accordance with Section 112.061 of the Florida Statutes
Description: The board is authorized to establish and maintain any hospital or related medical care facility for the use of the people of the district. Board members may employ necessary personnel.
Qualifications: Members shall be qualified electors and property owners who have resided in DeSoto County for more than 1 year prior to their appointment. Members shall not belong to the medical profession.

Jackson County Hospital Corporation

Authority: Chapter 76-389, Laws of Florida
Term: 4 years
Confirmation Required: None
Oversight: County Jurisdiction
Compensation: Per diem, in accordance with Section 112.061 of the Florida Statutes
Description: The commission provides revenue for the erection and maintenance of the Jackson Hospital.
Qualifications: Members shall be citizens and residents of Jackson County and shall reside in the hospital district served by the hospital corporation.

Lake Shore Hospital Authority of Columbia County

Authority: Chapter 72-509, Laws of Florida
Term: 4 years
Confirmation Required: None
Oversight: County Jurisdiction
Compensation: Per diem, in accordance with Section 112.061 of the Florida Statutes
Description: The Authority acquires and maintains the hospital and hospital facilities in Columbia County, sets rates, and charges for the services and facilities of hospitals and clinics.

Qualifications: The members shall be citizens and residents of Columbia County. No elected public official shall be a member of the board. One member shall be a practicing physician at Lake Shore Hospital.

Long-Term Care Ombudsman Councils, (19 district councils throughout the state)

Authority: Section 400.0069, Florida Statutes
Term: 3 years
Confirmation Required: None
Oversight: Department of Elderly Affairs
Compensation: Per diem, in accordance with Section 112.061 of the Florida Statutes
Description: The Committee serves as a third party for protecting the welfare and human rights of residents of a nursing home or long-term care facility, including determination of abuse and the resolution of complaints.
Qualifications: A council shall consist of 15 to 30 members. Any employee of the Agency for Health Care Administration and the Department of Children and Family Services or Elderly Affairs shall not serve on this council. Members shall be appointed by the council and approved by the governor within 30 days after their appointment.

Lower Florida Keys Hospital District, Monroe County

Authority: Chapter 77-605, Laws of Florida
Term: 4 years
Confirmation Required: None
Oversight: County Jurisdiction
Compensation: Per diem, in accordance with Section 112.061 of the Florida Statutes
Description: The board appoints necessary employees, fixes the compensation of all employees, and removes any employees or appointees. The board may borrow money in order to carry out all necessary provisions.

Qualifications: Members shall be qualified electors residing in the district for more than 1 year prior to their appointment. Members shall post bond before assuming office.

Madison County Health and Hospital Board

Authority: Chapter 67-1659, Laws of Florida
Term: 4 years
Confirmation Required: None
Oversight: County Jurisdiction
Compensation: Per diem, in accordance with Section 112.061 of the Florida Statutes
Description: The board has full and complete authority to work with any public health or hospital program which is beneficial to the people of Madison County.
Qualifications: Members shall be citizens of Madison County of mature judgment and experience, known to be public-spirited in the community.

Medicaid Pharmaceutical and Therapeutics Committee

Authority: Section 409.91195, Florida Statutes
Term: 2 years
Confirmation Required: None
Oversight: Agency for Health Care Administrator
Compensation: Per diem, in accordance with Section 112.061 of the Florida Statutes
Description: The committee develops a preferred drug formulary, pursuant to 42 USC 1396r-8. The committee reviews all drug classes included in the formulary at least every 12 months, and may recommend additions to and deletions from the formulary, so that the formulary provides medically appropriate drug therapies for Medicaid patients
Qualifications: The Committee shall consist of 11 members, each appointed by the governor. The governor shall ensure that at least some of the members represent Medicaid participating physicians and pharmacies. At least one member shall represent pharmaceutical manufacturers.

Office of Long-Term Care Policy Advisory Council

Authority: Section 430.041(4), Florida Statutes
Term: 4 years
Confirmation Required: None
Oversight: Department of Elderly Affairs
Compensation: Per diem, in accordance with Section 112.061 of the Florida Statutes
Description: The advisory council provides assistance and direction to the office, and ensures that the appropriate state agencies are properly implementing recommendations from that office.
Qualifications: The advisory council shall consist of 13 members, 5 appointed by the governor. The director of the Office of Long-Term Care Policy shall serve as the chairperson.

Practitioners Prescribing Patterns Advisory Panel

Authority: Chapter 99-393, Laws of Florida
Term: Pleasure of the Governor
Confirmation Required: None
Oversight: Department of Elderly Affairs
Compensation: Per diem, in accordance with Section 112.061 of the Florida Statutes
Description: The advisory panel is responsible for evaluating treatment guidelines and recommending ways to incorporate their use in the practice pattern identification program. Practitioners who are prescribing inappropriately or inefficiently, as determined by the agency, may have the prescribing of certain drugs subject to prior authorization.
Qualifications: The advisory panel shall consist of 9 members. The governor, the president of the senate, and the Speaker of the House shall each appoint 3 members to the panel.

Public Swimming and Bathing Facilities Advisory Review Board

Authority: Section 514.028, Florida Statutes
Term: 4 years

Confirmation Required: None
Oversight: Department of Health
Compensation: Per diem, in accordance with Section 112.061 of the Florida Statutes
Description: The board promotes better relations between swimming industries and the deptartment of health, makes recommendations on product standards, suggests means to protect the welfare of service users, and benefits the department of health by its experience and expertise.
Qualifications: Seven member shall be appointed by the governor. Members shall recommend agency action on variance requests, rules and policy developments, and other technical review problems.

Review Council for Biomedical and Social Research

Authority: Section 381.85(3) Florida Statutes
Term: 3 years
Confirmation Required: None
Oversight: Department of Legal Affairs
Compensation: Per diem, in accordance with Section 112.061 of the Florida Statutes
Description: The council provides a procedure by which proposed research on children or adults is supported with funds appropriated to the Department of Health, and by which the research can be efficiently and expeditiously assessed for compliance with the substantive and procedural requirements.
Qualifications: The governor, the president of the senate, and Speaker of the House shall each appoint 3 members to the council. Members shall not serve more than 2 consecutive terms. The chairperson shall be elected by the council.

South Lake County Hospital District Board of Trustees

Authority: Chapter 01-290, Laws of Florida
Term: 4 years
Confirmation Required: Senate

Oversight: County Jurisdiction
Compensation: Per diem, in accordance with Section 112.061 of the Florida Statutes
Description: This board is the governing body of the district and has exclusive control of all expenditures of the district. The board may employ a hospital director and such persons as may be required.
Qualifications: The board shall consist of 11 members, appointed by the governor. All members shall reside within the district.

Southeast Volusia Hospital District

Authority: Chapter 89-552, Laws of Florida
Term: 4 years
Confirmation Required: None
Oversight: County Jurisdiction
Compensation: Per diem, in accordance with Section 112.061 of the Florida Statutes
Description: Members maintain a hospital or hospitals as is necessary for the use of the people of the district. They appoint a superintendent and chief surgeon, borrow money, and issue notes.
Qualifications: Commissioners shall be qualified electors and property owners who reside in the district. Members shall post a bond before assuming office.

State Long-Term Care Ombudsman Council

Authority: Section 400.0067(3)(a), Florida Statutes
Term: 3 years
Confirmation Required: None
Oversight: Department of Elderly Affairs
Compensation: Per diem, in accordance with Section 112.061 of the Florida Statutes
Description: The council identifies, investigates, and resolves complaints made by, or on behalf of, residents of long-term care facilities. The council provides services to assist in protecting the health, safety, welfare, and rights of the residents.

Qualifications: The Council shall be composed of 15 members, 3 appointed by the governor. Appointments shall be made from a list submitted by the secretary of Elderly Affairs, in consultation with State Long-Term Care Ombudsman Council.

State of Florida Correctional Medical Authority

Authority: Section 945.602, Florida Statutes
Term: 4 years
Confirmation Required: Senate
Oversight: Department of Corrections
Compensation: Per diem, in accordance with Section 112.061 of the Florida Statutes
Description: The authority assists in the delivery of health care service for inmates in the Department of Corrections. It also advises the Department of Corrections on the professional conduct of primary, convalescent, dental, and mental health care providers. It also advises on quality care cost management.
Qualifications: The board shall be composed of 9 members appointed by the governor and confirmed by the senate.

Statewide Provider and Subscriber Assistance Program Panel

Authority: Section 408.7056(11) Florida Statutes
Term: 4 years
Confirmation Required: None
Oversight: Agency for Health Care Administration
Compensation: Per diem, in accordance with Section 112.061 of the Florida Statutes
Description: The agency adopts and implements a program to provide assistance to subscribers and providers, including those whose grievances are not resolved by the managed care entity to the satisfaction of the subscriber or provider. The panel meets in a timely manner to review, consider, hear grievances, and recommend to the agency or the department any action necessary concerning each case.

Qualifications: The panel shall consist both of members employed by the agency and members employed by the department, each chosen by their respective agencies. The panel shall also include a consumer and a physician appointed by the governor.

West Orange Healthcare District

Authority: Chapter 00-450, Laws of Florida
Term: 3 years
Confirmation Required: None
Oversight: County Jurisdiction
Compensation: Per diem, in accordance with Section 112.061 of the Florida Statutes
Description: The board is authorized and empowered to establish and maintain a hospital or hospitals necessary for the use of the people of the district.
Qualifications: There shall be 16 members. Nine shall be nominated from designated local organizations and 6 shall be nominated by the existing board.

Social Services / Community Affairs / Veterans Affairs

The boards, commissions and senior level appointments listed in this chapter deal with social service issues for Florida's families, communities, and individuals in need. Programs include economic self-sufficiency, family safety and preservation, and developmental services, as well as alcohol, drug abuse, and mental health services. They also help provide affordable housing for low and moderate income Floridians and assist in planning for responses to man-made and natural emergencies. They are dedicated to preventing unlawful discrimination, by ensuring that people in Florida are treated fairly and are given equal access to opportunities in employment, housing, and certain public accommodations. They may address the areas of employment discrimination, as well as discrimination in housing or other public services based on race, color, religion, sex, handicap, national origin, age, and marital status. Other areas of concern include: public guardianship programs and minority, women's, and veterans' advocacy programs and services.

Senior Level Appointments:

Secretary of the Department of Community Affairs
Secretary of the Department of Children and Families
Executive Director of the Department of Veterans' Affairs
Executive Director of the Statewide Public Guardianship
Executive Director of the State Office on Homelessness
Director of the Office of Urban Opportunity

Boards and Commissions:

Affordable Housing Study Commission

Authority: Section 420.609, Florida Statutes
Term: 4 years
Confirmation Required: None
Oversight: Department of Community Affairs
Compensation: Per diem, in accordance with Section 112.061 of the Florida Statutes
Description: The commission reviews, evaluates, and makes recommendations regarding housing programs and initiatives created since 1986, including the demographic study of farm workers, as required by Section 420.808. The commission provides recommendations in an annual report.
Qualifications: The governor shall appoint 21 members to staggered terms. See 93-181, the Laws of Florida, for revised membership qualification information.

Americans with Disabilities Act Working Group

Authority: Executive Order 99-80
Term: July 26, 2003
Confirmation Required: None
Oversight: Office of the governor

Compensation: Per diem, in accordance with Section 112.061 of the Florida Statutes

Description: The focus of the working group is to bring to all citizens of Florida full access to the resources, services, and opportunities to participate in all aspects of community life through the provision of appropriate accommodations. The mission of the working group is to provide information, referrals, education, and recommendations for compliance and implementation of the act.

Qualifications: The working group shall be comprised of no more than 15 members from both the public and private sector, appointed by the governor to serve at his or her pleasure. Fifty-one percent of the members shall be individuals protected under the act.

Board of Directors, Florida Healthy Kids Corporation

Authority: Section 624.91, Florida Statutes

Term: 3 years

Confirmation Required: None

Oversight: Department of Financial Services

Compensation: Per diem, in accordance with Section 112.061 of the Florida Statutes

Description: The directors organize school groups to facilitate the provision of preventive health care to children at no more than 4 sites. They also provide comprehensive health insurance coverage to children and their family members.

Qualifications: The governor shall appoint 5 of the 14 members. The state's chief financial officer (or his or her designee) shall chair the board. The board shall appoint an executive director.

Children's Services Councils (11): Alachua, Brevard, Broward, Charlotte, Collier, Hillsborough, Lee, Martin, Okeechobee, Palm Beach, Saint Lucie

Authority: See each Specific County Ordinance for each Specific County

Term: 4 years

Confirmation Required: None

Oversight: County Jurisdiction

Compensation: Per diem, in accordance with Section 112.061 of the Florida Statutes

Description: The council provides and maintains such preventive, developmental and rehabilitative treatment and services for children as it determines necessary. The council also allocates and provide funds for other agencies in the County which operate for the benefit of children.

Qualifications: The governor shall appoint 5 of the 10 members. The other 5 members shall include the superintendent of schools, a local school board member, the district administrator from the Department of Health, a county commissioner, and a judge. The board of county commissions shall submit 3 names to the governor for each vacancy. All members appointed shall have been a resident of the county for at least 24 months.

Commission on Responsible Fatherhood

Authority: Section 383.0113, Florida Statutes
Term: Pleasure of the Governor
Confirmation Required: None
Oversight: Department of Children and Family Services
Compensation: Per diem, in accordance with Section 112.061 of the Florida Statutes
Description: The purpose of the commission is to raise awareness of the problems created when a child grows up without the presence of a responsible father, to identify obstacles that impede or prevent the involvement of responsible fathers in the lives of their children; and to identify strategies that are successful in encouraging responsible fatherhood. The commission is encouraged to appoint subcommittees.

Qualifications: The commission shall be composed of 25 members, 7 appointed by the governor. The governor shall appoint the chairperson and the vice-chairperson.

Council on Homelessness

Authority: Section 420.622(2) Florida Statutes
Term: 2 years

Confirmation Required: None
Oversight: Department of Children and Family Services
Compensation: Per diem, in accordance with Section 112.061 of the Florida Statutes
Description: The council develops policy and advises The State Office on Homelessness. The council includes a report by December 31 of each year summarizing the council's recommendations to the office, the corresponding actions taken by the office, and any recommendations to the legislature for proposals to reduce homelessness in the state.
Qualifications: The council shall consist of 15 members, 4 appointed by the governor. The importance of minority, gender and geographic representation shall be considered when appointing members to the Council.

Family Care Councils (19 districts throughout the state).

Authority: Section 393.502, Florida Statutes
Term: 3 years
Confirmation Required: None
Oversight: Department of Children and Family Services
Compensation: Per diem, in accordance with Section 112.061 of the Florida Statutes
Description: The council assists in providing information and outreach to families, reviews the effectiveness of developmental services programs and make recommendations with respect to program implementation, and advises district developmental services administrators with respect to policy issues relevant to the community and family support system in the district.
Qualifications: The council shall consist of 10 to 15 members recommended by the district council and appointed by the governor. The governor shall make appointments within 45 days of receiving the recommendations. Members may serve only 2 consecutive terms.

Florida Commission on African-American Affairs

Authority: Section 14.27, Florida Statutes
Term: 4 years

Confirmation Required: None
Oversight: Office of the governor
Compensation: Per diem, in accordance with Section 112.061 of the Florida Statutes
Description: The commission develops specific strategies and plans to address the economic, social, educational, health, and welfare needs of African-Americans in the state. The commission also studies the changing and developing roles of African-Americans in American society. The commission may apply for and accept funds, grants, gifts, and services from the state, the federal government, or any other public or private source.
Qualifications: The commission shall consist of 15 members appointed by the governor. Members shall be of African-American origin and shall be professionally, socially and economically diverse. The governor shall appoint the chairperson from among the members of the commission.

Florida Commission on Community Service

Authority: Section 14.29, Florida Statutes
Term: 3 years
Confirmation Required: Senate
Oversight: Office of the governor
Compensation: Per diem, in accordance with Section 112.061 of the Florida Statutes
Description: The commission independently exercises the responsibilities required to comply with the terms and conditions of the National and Community Service Trust Act of 1993. The commission establishes policies and procedures relating to the expenditure of funds, in order to develop and facilitate community outreach initiatives.
Qualifications: The commission shall consist of no less than 15 and no more than 25 voting members, to be appointed on a bipartisan basis by the governor and confirmed by the senate. Any number of nonvoting members may be appointed by the governor. Not more than 50 percent plus 1, of the voting members shall be from the same political party.

Florida Commission on Human Relations

Authority: Section 760.03, Florida Statutes
Term: 4 years
Confirmation Required: Senate
Oversight: Office of the governor
Compensation: Per diem, in accordance with Section 112.061 of the Florida Statutes
Description: The commission promotes and encourages fair treatment and equal opportunity for all persons, regardless of race, color, religion, sex, national origin, age, handicap or marital status.
Qualifications: Twelve members shall be appointed by the governor. Members shall be broadly representative of various racial, religious, ethnic, social, economic, political, and professional groups within the state. Pursuant to Chapter 87-172 of the laws of Florida, at least 1 member shall be 60 years of age or older.

Florida Commission on the Status of Women

Authority: Section 14.24, Florida Statutes
Term: 4 years
Confirmation Required: Senate
Oversight: Office of Attorney General
Compensation: Per diem, in accordance with Section 112.061 of the Florida Statutes
Description: The commission studies the changing and developing roles of women in American society, including, but not limited to: the socio-economic factors that influence the status of women; the development of individual potential; the encouragement of women to utilize their capabilities and assume leadership roles, etc.
Qualifications: The governor shall appoint 3 of the 22 members. No member shall serve more than 8 consecutive years on the commission. Initial appointments and terms shall be staggered.

Florida Commission on Veterans' Affairs

Authority: Section 292.04, Florida Statutes
Term: 4 years
Confirmation Required: None
Oversight: Office of the governor
Compensation: Per diem, in accordance with Section 112.061 of the Florida Statutes
Description: The commission studies the problems and needs of Florida veterans and their dependents, acts as a liaison between veteran organizations and the state, and prepares an annual report by January 1.
Qualifications: Commissioners shall be war veterans with an honorable discharge. Eight members of this board shall be Florida citizens from regions that proportionally represent the veteran population within the states in Florida. The ninth member shall be from the state at large. Pursuant to Chapter 87-172 of the laws of Florida, at least 1 member shall be 60 years of age or older.

Florida Governor's Council on Indian Affairs, Inc.

Authority: Articles of Incorporation
Term: 3 Years
Confirmation Required: None
Oversight: Office of the governor
Compensation: Per diem, in accordance with Section 112.061 of the Florida Statutes
Description: This corporation is organized for the purpose of providing or helping to provide technical assistance for the educational, economic, social, and cultural advancement of the federally recognized tribes and their members within the state of Florida. It also provides information and assistance to the federal, state, and local government organizations, as well as to the general public.
Qualifications: The council shall consist of 15 members, 8 of whom must be representatives of the Florida Indian tribes. The Florida Indian members of the council shall include 4 members each from the Miccosukee and Seminole tribes.

Florida Housing Finance Corporation

Authority: Section 420.504, Florida Statutes
Term: 4 years
Confirmation Required: Senate
Oversight: Department of Community Affairs
Compensation: Per diem, in accordance with Section 112.061 of the Florida Statutes
Description: The corporation studies and analyzes housing needs within the state, seeking ways of meeting those needs upon request of the governor. It also participates in federal housing assistance programs.
Qualifications: A member who has a contract with Housing Finance Corporation or has an interest in a sponsor of Housing Finance Corporation shall give written disclosure of the relationship and be excused from any action relating to the contract or sponsor. The corporation board is composed of 9 members: 8 appointed by the governor with the secretary of of Community Affairs serving as an ex-officio member.

Florida Rehabilitation Council for the Blind

Authority: Section 413.011, Florida Statutes
Term: 3 years
Confirmation Required: None
Oversight: Department of Labor and Employment Security
Compensation: Per diem, in accordance with Section 112.061 of the Florida Statutes
Description: The council is created to assist the Department of Labor and Employment Security in the planning and development of statewide rehabilitation programs and services and to recommend improvements to such programs and services. The council supervises and evaluates such staff and other personnel as may be necessary to carry out its functions as consistent with law.
Qualifications: The council shall be composed of at least 13 members appointed by the governor. The governor shall select members after soliciting recommendations from organizations representing individuals who have disabilities, as well as organizations

interested in those individuals. Members shall serve 2 consecutive full terms.

Florida State Commission on Hispanic Affairs

Authority: Section 14.25, Florida Statutes
Term: 4 years
Confirmation Required: None
Oversight: Office of the governor
Compensation: Per diem, in accordance with Section 112.061 of the Florida Statutes
Description: The commission conducts an ongoing study of the problems and needs of those citizens of Florida who predominately speak the Spanish language. The commission prepares an annual report.
Qualifications: Members shall be broadly representative of the interests and needs of the persons in this State who are of Hispanic origin. Areas of study shall include education, social services, commerce, general culture, and the arts

Florida Statewide Advocacy Council

Authority: Section 402.165, Florida Statutes
Term: 4 years
Confirmation Required: None
Oversight: Department of Children and Family Services
Compensation: Per diem, in accordance with Section 112.061 of the Florida Statutes
Description: The council serves as a third-party mehcanism for protecting the constitutional and human rights of any client within a program or facility operated, funded, or regulated by any State agency.
Qualifications: The council shall consist of 15 residents of the state, one from each service area designated by the statewide council. Vacancies not filled by the governor in 60 days shall be filled by the Council. A member shall not serve more than 2 full consecutive terms.

Guardian Ad Litem Program Working Group

Authority: Executive Order 02-159
Term: September 15, 2002
Confirmation Required: None
Oversight: Office of the governor
Compensation: Per diem, in accordance with Section 112.061 of the Florida Statutes
Description: The working group is established to develop a recommended plan of action for realizing the full potential of the Guardian Ad Litem Program. The working group focuses on recommendations for actions, enhancing the effectiveness of the program in serving Florida's children, as well as enhancing efforts to recruit, train, and retain volunteer guardians.
Qualifications: The working group shall consist of 12 members appointed by the governor. Included in the group shall be 4 individuals recommended by the chief justice of the Florida Supreme Court. A chairperson shall be appointed by the governor.

Housing Authorities (21): Bradford, Brevard, Broward, Collier, Columbia, Flagler, Gilchrist, Hernando, Highlands, Indian, Lee, Levy, Manatee, Monroe, Nassau, Palm Beach, Pasco, Pinella, Seminole, Suwannee, and Union Counties

Authority: Section 421.27, Florida Statutes
Term: 4 years
Confirmation Required: None
Oversight: County Jurisdiction
Compensation: Per diem, in accordance with Section 112.061 of the Florida Statutes
Description: The authority acquires, leases and operates housing projects, and also provides for the construction, reconstruction, improvement, alteration, or repair of any housing project. The authority investigates dwelling and housing conditions that may be dangerous to the public.
Qualifications: The governor shall appoint 5 members who are qualified electors of the County. The appointments shall be

subject to approval by the board of county commissioners. Members shall not be an employee of the county. One member shall be a resident who is current in rent in a housing project or a person of low or very low income who resides within the housing authority's jurisdiction and is receiving rent subsidy through a program administered by the authority or public housing agency that has jurisdiction for the same locality served by the housing authority.

Housing Authority, Hardee County

Authority: County Resolution 97-35
Term: 4 years
Confirmation Required: None
Oversight: County Jurisdiction
Compensation: Per diem, in accordance with Section 112.061 of the Florida Statutes
Description: The housing authority provides for the construction, reconstruction, improvement, alteration or repair of dwelling units for the purpose of improving the state of affordable housing; holds or improves real property; acquired by gift, grant, bequest, devise or otherwise any property; and investigates into living, dwelling, and housing conditions, as well as the means and methods for improving such conditions.
Qualifications: The board shall consist of 7 members appointed by the governor. The governor shall appoint 1 commissioner who shall be a resident in a rental housing project, or who shall be a person of low income who is a recipient of a rent subsidy. No member shall be an employee of the county.

Housing Authority, Northwest Florida Region

Authority: Section 421.30, Florida Statutes
Term: 4 years
Confirmation Required: None
Oversight: Department of Community Affairs
Compensation: Per diem, in accordance with Section 112.061 of the Florida Statutes

Description: The authority has the power to acquire and operate housing projects, to arrange for services in connection with a housing project, and to lease or rent any structures embraced in any housing project.
Qualifications: No member shall acquire an interest in any housing project. There shall be an odd number of members, and at least one member shall be appointed from each county in the housing authority.

Human Rights Advocacy Committees, (35 committees throughout the state)

Authority: Section 402.166, Florida Statutes
Term: 4 years
Confirmation Required: None
Oversight: Department of Children and Family Services
Compensation: Per diem, in accordance with Section 112.061 of the Florida Statutes
Description: The committee serves as a third-party mechanism for protecting the constitutional and human rights of any departmental client within a program or facility operated, funded, licensed, or regulated by the Department of Human Rights Services.
Qualifications: No fewer than 7 members and no more than 15 members may serve 2 consecutive terms. Vacancies shall be filled by the committee, subject to the governor's approval.

One Church, One Child of Florida Corporation

Authority: Section 409.1755, Florida Statutes
Term: 3 years
Confirmation Required: None
Oversight: Department of Children and Family Services
Compensation: Per diem, in accordance with Section 112.061 of the Florida Statutes
Description: The corporation provides services to assist in the adoption of African-American children, participates in charity

work, involves persons with religious and clerical expertise, provides literacy and educational guidelines, and promotes child welfare.

Qualifications: The board of directors shall consist of 31 members appointed by the governor. Two members shall be from each service district of Department of Children and Family and member-at-large. The board shall appoint the executive director.

Statewide Drug Policy Advisory Council

Authority: Section 397.333, Florida Statutes
Term: 4 years
Confirmation Required: None
Oversight: Office of the governor
Compensation: Per diem, in accordance with Section 112.061 of the Florida Statutes
Description: The council conducts a comprehensive analysis of the problem of substance abuse in this state and makes recommendations to the governor and the legislature for developing and implementing a state drug-control strategy. The council makes recommendations for funding substance-abuse programs and services, and also reviews different methodologies for evaluating such programs.
Qualifications: The council shall consist of 25 members, 11 appointed by the governor. Members shall have professional or occupational expertise in issues that relate to drug enforcement and substance-abuse programs and services.

Planning & Oversight / Federal, State & Regional Concerns / Military

The boards, commissions and executive level appointments listed in this chapter deal with issues that provide planning and guidance for federal, state, and regional concerns, including financial planning, growth management, along with the oversight of the state employees' retirement fund, and monitoring of federal and state elections. The National Guard and the emergency response systems are included in this section, as well as international trade issues and planning concerns for regional projects that enhance the quality of life for all Floridians.

In addition to the appointments mentioned in this chapter, the governor may fill vacancies due to resignation, death, removal, promotion or other special circumstances, including appointments to federal, state and locally elected offices. Other offices which the governor may appoint to in the case of vacancy include: taxation, lighting, and municipal services districts, for which the membership is elected by the public.

Senior Level Appointments

Secretary of the Department of State
Secretary of the Department of Management Services
Adjutant General of the Department of Military Affairs
Executive Director of the State Board of Administration
Executive Director of the Department of Revenue
Director of the State Technology Office / CIO

Boards and Commissions:

Baker County Development Commission

Authority: Chapter 00-442, Laws of Florida
Term: 4 years
Confirmation Required: None
Oversight: County Jurisdiction
Compensation: Per diem, in accordance with Section 112.061 of the Florida Statutes
Description: The commission is created for the purpose of performing such acts as are necessary for the planning and development of Baker County.
Qualifications: The commission shall be composed of 7 members appointed by the governor. There shall be 1 member from each district within the county and 2 at-large members. At least 2 of the members shall be women.

Board of Supervisors, Miami-Dade County Community Improvement Trust

Authority: Chapter 00-348, Laws of Florida
Term: 4 years
Confirmation Required: None
Oversight: County Jurisdiction
Compensation: Per diem, in accordance with Section 112.061 of the Florida Statutes

Description: The board takes all steps which are reasonable and necessary to generate local support for the development of projects, including professional sports facilities and related amenities and infrastructure. The board also serves as an intermediary and facilitates negotiations with and among private interests, community organizations, and governmental authorities in connection with the construction or development of such projects.

Qualifications: The board shall be composed of 9 members. Two members shall be appointed by the governor, and 3 members shall be appointed by the county commission. The city and county mayor shall each appoint 1 member, and 2 members shall be appointed by the city commission with the largest population.

Bradford County Development Authority

Authority: Chapter 61-1894, Laws of Florida
Term: 4 years
Confirmation Required: None
Oversight: County Jurisdiction
Compensation: Per diem, in accordance with Section 112.061 of the Florida Statutes
Description: The Authority is created (as a body corporate and politic) for the purpose of performing such acts as shall be necessary for the sound planning and development of Bradford County.
Qualifications: Members shall be freeholders and qualified electors of the County. Members shall be appointed upon recommendation from the Starke–Bradford County Chamber of Commerce.

Civil Service Board of Escambia County

Authority: Chapter 79-453, Laws of Florida
Term: 4 years
Confirmation Required: Senate
Oversight: County Jurisdiction
Compensation: Per diem, in accordance with Section 112.061 of the Florida Statutes

Description: The board is authorized to prescribe standard policies for the administration of pay plans and other conditions related to employment of those positions, under the career civil service system.

Qualifications: Board members shall be public-spirited persons of recognized standing and have known interest in the improvement of public administration. No member shall be employed or have been an employee within the year prior to appointment, in any capacity by any agency covered by the Escambia County Civil Service System.

Clay County Development Authority

Authority: Chapter 72-504, Laws of Florida
Term: 4 years
Confirmation Required: None
Oversight: County Jurisdiction
Compensation: Per diem, in accordance with Section 112.061 of the Florida Statutes
Description: The authority is to perform such acts as necessary for the sound planning and development of Clay County.
Qualifications: The governor shall appoint 10 lay members who are freeholders and qualified electors of Clay County.

Commission on Ethics

Authority: Section 112.321, Florida Statutes
Term: 2 years
Confirmation Required: Senate
Oversight: State Legislature
Compensation: Per diem, in accordance with Section 112.061 of the Florida Statutes
Description: The commission receives and investigates complaints concerning the conduct of officers and employees of the state, county, city, or other political subdivisions of the state.
Qualifications: Five members shall be appointed by the governor, of which no more than 3 appointees shall be from the same political party. No member shall hold any public employment or serve more than 2 full terms. One member shall be a former city or County official.

Committee to Review the State Comprehensive Plan

Authority: Section 186.007(9), Florida Statutes
Term: Pleasure of the Governor
Confirmation Required: None
Oversight: Office of the governor
Compensation: Per diem, in accordance with Section 112.061 of the Florida Statutes
Description: The committee reviews and makes recommendations regarding revisions to the state comprehensive plan which is to be considered for inclusion in the governor's recommendations to the administration commission, pursuant to Section 186.008(1). In reviewing the goals and policies relating to growth and development, the committee considers the plan guidelines set forth in Section 186.009.
Qualifications: The governor shall appoint a committee consisting of persons from both the public and private sectors who represent the broad range of interests covered by the state comprehensive plan; this includes state, regional, and local government representatives.

Department of Financial Services Committee of Transition Management

Authority: Chapter 02-404, Laws of Florida
Term: Pleasure of the Governor
Confirmation Required: None
Oversight: Office of the governor
Compensation: Per diem, in accordance with Section 112.061 of the Florida Statutes
Description: The Committee oversees the transition to the new Department of Financial Services and the new Financial Services Commission. The duties include providing a written report that specifies the placement of those positions that are transferred to the chief financial officer, the Department of Financial Services, and the offices of the Financial Services Commission.

Qualifications: The governor, the comptroller, the treasurer, the chair of the house fiscal responsibility council, and the chair of the senate appropriations committee shall each appoint one member to the committee.

Eastpoint Water and Sewer District

Authority: Chapter 67-1399, Laws of Florida
Term: 4 years
Confirmation Required: None
Oversight: County Jurisdiction
Compensation: Per diem, in accordance with Section 112.061 of the Florida Statutes
Description: The purpose of the board is to acquire, operate, and maintain waterworks or sewage facilities within the territorial limits of the district, and to fix and collect rates for services furnished.
Qualifications: Members shall be freeholders and qualified electors of the district, as well as citizens of the United States. Each member shall post a bond before assuming office.

Florida Communities Trust

Authority: Section 380.504, Florida Statutes
Term: 4 years
Confirmation Required: Senate
Oversight: Department of Community Affairs
Compensation: Per diem, in accordance with Section 112.061 of the Florida Statutes
Description: The governing body makes and executes contracts and other instruments necessary or convenient to the exercise of the powers of the trust. It provides technical and financial assistance to local and state governments, water management district, regional planning council, and non-profit agencies.
Qualifications: The governing body shall consist of 5 members, 4 appointed by the governor. The secretary of community affairs serves as chairperson. The secretary of the Department of Environmental Protection shall also serve.

Florida Elections Commission

Authority: Chapter 106.24, Florida Statutes
Term: 4 years
Confirmation Required: Senate
Oversight: Department of State
Compensation: Per diem, in accordance with Section 112.061 of the Florida Statutes
Description: The commission has jurisdiction to investigate and determine violations of the State election laws, refer matters to the State attorneys, record hearings, and impose civil penalties by fines.
Qualifications: The governor shall appoint a chairperson for a maximum of 4 years concurrent with the governor's term in office. Eight members shall be appointed from a list of nominees submitted by the senate president, the Speaker, and the senate and house minority leaders. Only 5 members shall be from the same political party. Members may serve no more than 2 full terms.

Florida Geographic Information Advisory Council

Authority: Section 282.404(6) Florida Statutes
Term: 4 years
Confirmation Required: None
Oversight: State Technology Office
Compensation: Per diem, in accordance with Section 112.061 of the Florida Statutes
Description: The council provides technical assistance and recommendations to the board. The council makes recommendations to the board for policies, procedures, standards, and technical solutions pertaining to the planning, coordination sharing, consistency, development, and maintenance of geographic information. The council also develops operational procedures for the conduct of business.
Qualifications: The council shall consist of 27 members, 12 appointed by the governor, 3 of whom must have technical expertise

in geographic information issues. The governor shall make recommendations from nominees supplied by the respective organization. Federal officers may serve as ex officio members.

Florida Legislative Committee on Intergovernmental Relations

Authority: Section 11.70(3) Florida Statutes
Term: 2 years
Confirmation Required: None
Oversight: State Legislature
Compensation: Per diem, in accordance with Section 112.061 of the Florida Statutes
Description: The purpose of the committee is to improve coordination and cooperation among state and local governments, other states, and the federal government. The committee studies problems of the intergovernmental aspects of governmental structure, finance, functional performance, and relationships at the local, regional, state and interstate levels. The committee recommends solutions to intergovernmental problems.
Qualifications: The committee shall be composed of 15 members. Seven members shall be appointed by the governor from elected and appointed state and local officials, as well as from other interested citizens, for a 2 year term. The terms shall run from general election to general election, and members may be reappointed.

Florida National Guard, General Officers

Authority: Section 250.13, Florida Statutes
Term: Pleasure of the Governor
Confirmation Required: Senate
Oversight: Federal Organization Titles
Compensation: Per diem, in accordance with Section 112.061 of the Florida Statutes
Description: Officers may serve until the age of 64.
Qualifications: The appointment of officers in the National Guard shall be made by the governor in accordance with the laws of the military.

Governor's Cuba Advisory Group

Authority: Executive Order 96-150
Term: Pleasure of the Governor
Confirmation Required: None
Oversight: Office of the governor
Compensation: Per diem, in accordance with Section 112.061 of the Florida Statutes
Description: The advisory group serves as an "information liaison" with Florida's communities, sharing pertinent information on US/Cuba policy. The advisory group focuses on the issues of immigration, commerce, and tourism. In addition to these areas of study, the advisory group is empowered to examine any other relevant issues, as directed from time to time by the governor.
Qualifications: The advisory group shall consist of 15 members appointed by the governor to serve at his or her pleasure. Members shall represent governmental interests, private enterprise, humanitarian agencies, and academic organizations. Federal officials are ex officio members.

Hamilton County Development Authority

Authority: Chapter 61-2217, Laws of Florida
Term: 4 years
Confirmation Required: None
Oversight: County Jurisdiction
Compensation: Per diem, in accordance with Section 112.061 of the Florida Statutes
Description: The authority is created for the purpose of performing such acts as are necessary for the sound planning and development of Hamilton County.
Qualifications: Members shall be property owners and qualified electors of the County.

Hillsborough County Civil Service Board

Authority: Chapter 96-519, Laws of Florida
Term: 4 years

Confirmation Required: Senate
Oversight: County Jurisdiction
Compensation: Per diem, in accordance with Section 112.061 of the Florida Statutes
Description: The board makes recommendations and sets rules on employment, classification and pay plans, and all matters relating to employees of the civil service system in Hillsborough County.
Qualifications: Members shall be qualified electors and shall not be a public officer or an employee of any employing authority.

Immokalee Water and Sewer District, Collier County

Authority: Chapter 98-495, Laws of Florida
Term: 4 years
Confirmation Required: None
Oversight: County Jurisdiction
Compensation: Per diem, in accordance with Section 112.061 of the Florida Statutes
Description: The district acquires, purchases, constructs, improves, maintains, and operates any water system or sewer system serving unincorporated areas, as well as other customers and users.
Qualifications: Members of the board shall be qualified electors of the district and citizens of the United States. Members shall be appointed by the governor.

Investment Advisory Council

Authority: Section 215.444, Florida Statutes
Term: 4 years
Confirmation Required: Senate
Oversight: Federal Organization Titles
Compensation: Per diem, in accordance with Section 112.061 of the Florida Statutes
Description: The council reviews the investments made by the staff of the board of administration and makes recommendations to the board regarding investment policy, strategy, and procedures.

Qualifications: Members shall possess special knowledge, experience, and familiarity with financial investments and portfolio management.

Lawton Chiles Endowment Fund Advisory Council

Authority: Section 215.5601(6) Florida Statutes
Term: 4 years
Confirmation Required: None
Oversight: Department of Children and Family Services
Compensation: Per diem, in accordance with Section 112.061 of the Florida Statutes
Description: The advisory council reviews the funding priorities of the state agencies, evaluates their requests according to the mission and goals of the agencies and the legislative intent for the use of endowment funds, and allows for public input and advocacy.
Qualifications: The council shall consist of 15 members, 8 appointed by the governor.

National Conference of Commissioners on Uniform State Laws

Authority: Section 13.10, Florida Statutes
Term: 4 years
Confirmation Required: Senate
Oversight: Federal Organization Titles
Compensation: Per diem, in accordance with Section 112.061 of the Florida Statutes
Description: The board ascertains the best means to effect assimilation and uniformity in the laws of the state. It also cooperates and advises with similar commissions in other states.
Qualifications: The governor shall appoint, subject to confirmation by the senate, 3 commissioners to the National Conference of Commissioners on Uniform State Laws. Florida residents, who because of long service in the cause of the uniformity of state legislation shall have been elected life members, shall also serve as Florida's representatives to the national conference.

Regional Planning Councils (11): Apalachee, Central, East Central, North Central, Northeast, South, Southwest, Tampa Bay, Treasure Coast, West, and Withlacoochee Regions

Authority: Section 186.504, Florida Statutes
Term: 3 years
Confirmation Required: Senate
Oversight: Department of Community Affairs
Compensation: Per diem, in accordance with Section 112.061 of the Florida Statutes
Description: The council acts in an advisory capacity to its local planning district, conducts local resource studies, adopts comprehensive regional policy plans, and prepares disaster preparation plans and annual reports.
Qualifications: One-third of the council members shall be appointed by the governor. No two members shall reside in the same county, until each county is represented. The governor's appointees may be locally elected officials or laypersons. Local governments shall appoint the remaining members of the council.

Saint Lucie County Fire District

Authority: Chapter 96-532, Laws of Florida
Term: 2 years
Confirmation Required: None
Oversight: County Jurisdiction
Compensation: Per diem, in accordance with Section 112.061 of the Florida Statutes
Description: The board may acquire fire-fighting equipment and also employ necessary personnel to protect the properties located in the district.
Qualifications: The governor shall appoint 1 member to the board.

State Emergency Response Commission

Authority: Executive Order 98-153
Term: Pleasure of the Governor
Confirmation Required: None

Oversight: Department of Community Affairs
Compensation: Per diem, in accordance with Section 112.061 of the Florida Statutes
Description: The commission is responsible for supervising the state's compliance with Title III of the Federal Superfund Amendments and Reauthorization Act of 1986.
Qualifications: Members shall b representatives of state agencies and private organizations.

Taxation and Budget Reform Commission

Authority: Article XI, Section 6, Florida Constitution
Term: Pleasure of the Governor
Confirmation Required: None
Oversight: Governor, President of the Senate and Speaker of the House
Compensation: Per diem, in accordance with Section 112.061 of the Florida Statutes
Description: The commission reviews matters relating to state and local taxation and the budgetary process, issues a report, proposes statutory changes to the legislature as needed and submits proposed constitutional changes to the voters. The commission will adopt its rules of procedure.
Qualifications: The governor shall appoint 11 of the 29 members. The president of the senate and the Speaker of the House shall each appoint 7 members plus 2 non-voting ex officio legislative members. The commission members shall elect the chairperson.

Wireless 911 Board

Authority: Section 365.172(5)(a) Florida Statutes
Term: 4 years
Confirmation Required: None
Oversight: Department of Management Services
Compensation: Per diem, in accordance with Section 112.061 of the Florida Statutes

Description: The wireless 911 board is established to administer the E911 fee imposed on subscribers. This includes receiving revenues derived from the fee; distributing portions of such revenue to providers, counties, and the department; accounting for receipts, distributions, and income derived by the funds maintained in the fund; and providing annual reports to the governor and the legislature.

Qualifications: The board shall consist of 7 members, 6 appointed by the governor. The system directors of the Division of Communications and the Department of Management Services, shall serve on the board. Not more than one member shall be appointed to represent any single provider on the board. Members may serve 2 terms.

Transportation /
Highway Safety &
Motor Vehicles /
Public Utilities

The boards, commissions and senior level appointments listed in this chapter work to provide a safe, interconnected statewide transportation system for Florida's citizens and visitors that ensures the mobility of people and goods. Enhancing Florida's quality of life by facilitating efficient, safe and reliable utility services at fair prices are among the many duties of the board and commissions described here. Another goal is providing economic development for the state through the support of space-related business and educational activities. The Florida space authority helps the state to maintain its position as the world's leading location for space enterprise and training.

In addition to the appointments mentioned in this chapter, the governor may fill vacancies due to resignation, death, removal, promotion or other special circumstances, including appointments to elected positions on: port authorities, river/water management districts, road and bridge districts, waterway and beach districts, and airport authorities.

Senior Level Appointments:

Secretary of the Department of Transportation
Executive Director of the Department of Highway Safety and Motor Vehicles
Chair of the Public Service Commission

Boards and Commissions:

Board of Directors of the Florida Commercial Space Financing

Authority: Section 331.411, Florida Statutes
Term: 3 years
Confirmation Required: None
Oversight: Spaceport Florida Authority
Compensation: Per diem, in accordance with Section 112.061 of the Florida Statutes
Description: The purpose of the corporation is to expand employment and income opportunities for residents of the state by providing businesses domiciled in the state with information, technical assistance, and financial assistance, in order to support space-related transactions; this will increase the development within the state of commercial aerospace products, activities, services and facilities.
Qualifications: The board of directors shall consist of 7 members, plus 2 ex officio nonvoting members. The governor shall appoint 2 members. All members shall be residents of the state. The board shall appoint a president of the corporation.

Board of Supervisors, Florida Space Authority

Authority: Section 331.308, Florida Statutes
Term: 4 years
Confirmation Required: Senate
Oversight: Office of the governor
Compensation: Per diem, in accordance with Section 112.061 of the Florida Statutes

Description: The board has powers to engage in the planning and implementation of space-related economic and educational development within the state, adopt bylaws, and adopt administration rules and regulations with respect to any projects of the authority, with notice and public hearing.

Qualifications: The board shall consist of 8 members who are residents of the state, appointed by the governor. The Speaker of the House shall appoint a member of the house of representatives and the senate president shall appoint a member of the senate, both shall serve as ex-officio nonvoting members. The lieutenant governor shall serve as the chairperson.

Carrabelle–Franklin Port and Airport Authority

Authority: Chapter 86-464, Laws of Florida
Term: 4 years
Confirmation Required: None
Oversight: County Jurisdiction
Compensation: Per diem, in accordance with Section 112.061 of the Florida Statutes
Description: The authority is responsible for formulating and carrying out plans for the long-range development of port facilities, recreational facilities, airports facilities, and traffic through such facilities.
Qualifications: The city commission shall appoint 4 members from the local area. The governor shall appoint 3 members to represent regional interests, from lists furnished by a nominating committee. The authority shall fill all other vacancies.

Central Florida Regional Transportation Authority

Authority: Section 343.63, Florida Statutes
Term: 4 years
Confirmation Required: None
Oversight: Department of Transportation
Compensation: Per diem, in accordance with Section 112.061 of the Florida Statutes

Description: The authority establishes and determines policies as is necessary, for the operation and promotion of a commuter rail system. It also adopts rules, as is necessary, to govern the operation of a commercial rail system and commercial rail facilities.
Qualifications: The authority shall consist of 9 members. The governor shall appoint 2 members. The county commission of Seminole, Orange and Osceola Counties shall each elect a commissioner. The secretary of transportation shall appoint the district secretary, or a designee for such person.

Clay County Utility Authority

Authority: Chapter 94-491, Laws of Florida
Term: 3 years
Confirmation Required: None
Oversight: County Jurisdiction
Compensation: Per diem, in accordance with Section 112.061 of the Florida Statutes
Description: The authority is created for the purpose of acquiring, constructing, financing, owning, managing, providing, promoting, improving, expanding, maintaining, operating, regulating, franchising, and otherwise having plenary authority, with respect to certain utility systems within the territorial limits of Clay County and areas adjacent thereto. All powers with respect to water and sewer lie within the authority.
Qualifications: The board of supervisors shall consist of 7 members, 1 appointed by the governor. The board members shall serve no more than 2 consecutive 3 year terms. All board members shall be qualified electors and ratepayers of Clay County.

Commission for the Transportation Disadvantaged

Authority: Section 427.012, Florida Statutes
Term: 4 years
Confirmation Required: None
Oversight: Department of Transportation
Compensation: Per diem, in accordance with Section 112.061 of the Florida Statutes

Description: The council will foster the coordination of transportation services to the transportation disadvantaged by establishing statewide objectives for providing such services.
Qualifications: The governor shall appoint 6 of the 27 members for 4 year terms. The secretary of transportation, the commissioner of education, the secretary of the Department of Health, the secretary of Labor and Employment Security and the executive director of Veterans Affairs or their designee shall serve on the commission. The president of the Florida Association for Community Action shall also serve.

Emerald Coast Bridge Authority

Authority: Chapter 01-346, Laws of Florida
Term: 4 years
Confirmation Required: None
Oversight: County Jurisdiction
Compensation: Per diem, in accordance with Section 112.061 of the Florida Statutes
Description: The authority plans for and studies the feasibility of constructing, operating, and maintaining a bridge or bridges transversing the Choctawhatchee Bay and/or Santa Rosa Sound, as well as access roads to said bridge(s).
Qualifications: The authority shall consist of 5 members appointed by the governor. Not less than 3 members shall be residents of the area extending west from East Pass bridge to the boundary line between Santa Rosa and Okaloosa County and north to Eglin Reserve. Terms shall expire on June 30 each year.

Escambia County Interstate 110 Extension Authority

Authority: County Resolution R99-194
Term: 4 years
Confirmation Required: Senate
Oversight: County Jurisdiction
Compensation: Per diem, in accordance with Section 112.061 of the Florida Statutes

Description: The authority may acquire, hold, construct, improve, maintain, operate, own, and lease an expressway system. Construction of an expressway system may be completed in segments, phases or stages. The authority may construct any extensions of, additions to, or improvements to the expressway system or appurtenant facilities, including approaches, roads, bridges, and avenues of access.

Qualifications: The authority shall consist of 10 members, 2 appointed by the governor. Each member shall be a permanent resident of the county.

Escambia County Utilities Authority

Authority: Chapter 92-248, Laws of Florida
Term: 4 years
Confirmation Required: None
Oversight: County Jurisdiction
Compensation: Per diem, in accordance with Section 112.061 of the Florida Statutes
Description: The authority is created for the purpose of acquiring, constructing, financing, owning, managing, providing, promoting, improving, expanding, maintaining, operating, regulating, franchising, and otherwise having plenary authority with respect to certain utility systems within the territorial limits of Escambia County.

Qualifications: The authority shall consist of 7 members, who shall each be an elector of Escambia County. The governor shall be appointed to fill positions when a vacancy occurs. The successor shall be a resident of the district in which the vacancy occurred.

Expressway Authority of Broward County

Authority: Section 348.242, Florida Statutes
Term: 4 years
Confirmation Required: Senate
Oversight: County Jurisdiction

Compensation: Per diem, in accordance with Section 112.061 of the Florida Statutes
Description: The authority shall acquire, hold, construct, improve, maintain, operate, own, and lease the Broward County Expressway System. The authority shall construct necessary additions, improvements, and facilities.
Qualifications: Members shall be permanent residents of Broward County. Two members shall be appointed by the governor and 3 members shall be appointed by the board of county commissioners.

Florida High-Speed Rail Authority

Authority: Section 341.821, Florida Statutes
Term: 4 years
Confirmation Required: None
Oversight: Department of Transportation
Compensation: Per diem, in accordance with Section 112.061 of the Florida Statutes
Description: The authority plans, administers, and manages the preliminary engineering and preliminary environmental assessment of the intrastate high-speed rail system in the state.
Qualifications: The governing board of the authority shall consist of 10 members. The governor, the president of the senate and the Speaker of the House shall each appoint 3 members. The secretary of transportation shall be a non-voting ex officio member of the board.

Florida Highway Beautification Council

Authority: Section 339.2405, Florida Statutes
Term: 4 years
Confirmation Required: None
Oversight: Department of Transportation
Compensation: Per diem, in accordance with Section 112.061 of the Florida Statutes

Description: The council accepts, reviews, prioritizes, and makes recommendations for grant awards to local government programs for the purpose of highway beautification. The council also provides information to local programs and recommends funding.
Qualifications: See specific districts for qualification information. All members shall be residents of the state. Members shall serve at the pleasure of the governor. The governor shall appoint the first chairperson.

Florida Public Service Commission

Authority: Section 350.01, Florida Statutes
Term: 4 years
Confirmation Required: Senate
Oversight: Public Service Commission
Compensation: $122,948.00 per year + per diem, in accordance with Section 112.061 of the Florida Statutes
Description: The commission is responsible for regulating the rates, services, and safety of privately owned public utilities, as well as adopting energy efficiency goals.
Qualifications: The commissioners shall not have any interest in any railroad or utility. Vacancies shall be filled from a list of no less than 3 persons per vacancy, which shall be recommended by the public services commission nominating council to the governor.

Florida Transportation Commission

Authority: Section 20.23, Florida Statutes
Term: 4 years
Confirmation Required: Senate
Oversight: Department of Transportation
Compensation: Per diem, in accordance with Section 112.061 of the Florida Statutes
Description: The commission serves as a review board for current transportation policies and recommends future improvements to the governor and the legislature. The commission also oversees activities of the Department of Transportation through review of budget and policy.

Qualifications: Members shall represent all geographic areas of the state. Each member shall be a registered voter and a citizen of the state, possess private sector business managerial experience, and represent the needs of the state as a whole.

Gainesville-Alachua County Regional Airport Authority

Authority: Chapter 95-457, Laws of Florida
Term: 3 years
Confirmation Required: None
Oversight: County Jurisdiction
Compensation: Per diem, in accordance with Section 112.061 of the Florida Statutes
Description: The authority has jurisdiction over the operation, maintenance, and improvements to the airport and airport facilities.
Qualifications: The governor shall appoint 3 of the 9 members. Members shall reside within the city or county and shall not hold any elected office. No person who has transacted business with the authority is eligible for appointment until 3 years after the last transaction.

Governor's Council for Young Adult Drivers

Authority: Executive Order 95-295
Term: Pleasure of the Governor
Confirmation Required: None
Oversight: Department of Transportation
Compensation: Per diem, in accordance with Section 112.061 of the Florida Statutes
Description: The council has authority to establish regional advisory groups, made up of student members from each of the schools districts within the regions. The council researches and evaluates the problems of automobile accidents in which young adult drivers are involved. The council may coordinate its efforts with the Partners for Highway Safety Foundation, a Florida not-for-profit corporation.

Qualifications: The council shall be appointed by and serve at the pleasure of the governor. The council shall consist of students and young adults. Members shall be appointed to represent several state agencies with responsibility to assist in the education of youthful drivers.

Greater Orlando Aviation Authority

Authority: Chapter 98-492, Laws of Florida
Term: 4 years
Confirmation Required: Senate
Oversight: County Jurisdiction
Compensation: Per diem, in accordance with Section 112.061 of the Florida Statutes
Description: The authority constructs, acquires and improves any facilities for handling passengers, mail, express, and freight aircraft.
Qualifications: The authority shall consist of 7 members, 5 appointed by the governor. The city council and the county commission shall each appoint 1 member. No person shall serve more than 2 consecutive terms or 8 consecutive years.

Harbor Master for Port of Fort Pierce, Saint Lucie County

Authority: Section 313.01, Florida Statutes
Term: 4 years
Confirmation Required: Senate
Oversight: County Jurisdiction
Compensation: Per diem, in accordance with Section 112.061 of the Florida Statutes
Description: The harbor master regulates and stations the wharves to vessels arriving at the port, remove vessels not receiving or discharging cargoes, and has the power to determine the duty of masters of vessels.
Qualifications: Harbor masters shall exist in counties with populations of less than 300,000 and shall post a bond set in the amount for ports in general or for certain specified ports.

Hillsborough Area Regional Transit Authority

Authority: Section 163.567, Florida Statutes
Term: 3 years
Confirmation Required: None
Oversight: County Jurisdiction
Compensation: Per diem, in accordance with Section 112.061 of the Florida Statutes
Description: The authority plans, finances, acquires, constructs, operates, and maintains mass transit facilities.
Qualifications: The authority shall consist of 11 members, 2 appointed by the governor.

Hillsborough County Aviation Authority

Authority: Chapter 83-424, Laws of Florida
Term: 4 years
Confirmation Required: None
Oversight: County Jurisdiction
Compensation: Per diem, in accordance with Section 112.061 of the Florida Statutes
Description: The Authority has exclusive jurisdiction, control, supervision, and management over all airports in the county. The authority may lease any airport or employ any personnel required to carry out its duties.
Qualifications: The governor shall appoint 3 of the 5 members. One member shall be the mayor of Tampa. The final member shall be appointed by the county commission and must reside in, but not work for, Hillsborough County.

Jacksonville Airport Authority

Authority: Chapter 01-319, Laws of Florida
Term: 4 years
Confirmation Required: Senate
Oversight: Local Government Jurisdiction

Compensation: Per diem, in accordance with Section 112.061 of the Florida Statutes
Description: The authority operates, manages, and controls all publicly owned airports and ancillary facilities located within Duval County. The powers that relate to aviation issues in Duval County are vested in the Jacksonville Airport Authority.
Qualifications: The authority shall consist of 7 members, 4 appointed by the governor. The mayor of the city of Jacksonville shall appoint 3 members. Members may serve only 2 consecutive full terms.

Jacksonville Seaport Authority

Authority: Chapter 01-319, Laws of Florida
Term: 4 years
Confirmation Required: Senate
Oversight: Local Government Jurisdiction
Compensation: Per diem, in accordance with Section 112.061 of the Florida Statutes
Description: The authority operates, manages, and controls the seaport and ancillary facilities located within Duval County. The powers that relate to maritime issues in Duval County are vested in the Jacksonville Seaport Authority.
Qualifications: The authority shall consist of 7 members, 3 appointed by the governor. The mayor of the city of Jacksonville shall appoint 4 members. Members may serve only 2 consecutive full terms.

Jacksonville Transportation Authority

Authority: Section 349.03, Florida Statutes
Term: 4 years
Confirmation Required: Senate
Oversight: County Jurisdiction
Compensation: Per diem, in accordance with Section 112.061 of the Florida Statutes

Description: The authority formulates and implements a plan for a mass transit system in Jacksonville, maintains and operates the Jacksonville Expressway System, submits annual requests for funds, issues bonds, and receives bids.
Qualifications: Three members shall be appointed by the governor. Members shall be residents and qualified electors of the city of Jacksonville, with the exception of the Department of Transportation engineer.

Metropolitan Planning Organization of Miami–Dade County

Authority: Section 339.175, Florida Statutes
Term: 4 years
Confirmation Required: None
Oversight: Department of Transportation
Compensation: Per diem, in accordance with Section 112.061 of the Florida Statutes
Description: The organization is responsible for the development of a transportation improvement program in order to initiate federally aided transportation facilities. The organization is also responsible for transportation related air, noise, and water-quality planning within urbanized areas assigned by federal and state laws.
Qualifications: The governor shall appoint 4 voting members. One member shall be an elected official from a municipality within the county and 1member shall be a layperson who does not hold an elected office and who resides in the unincorporated portion of the county.

Miami–Dade County Expressway Authority

Authority: Section 348.003, Florida Statutes
Term: 4 years
Confirmation Required: None
Oversight: County Jurisdiction
Compensation: Per diem, in accordance with Section 112.061 of the Florida Statutes

Description: The authority is created and established pursuant to the Florida Expressway Act, and may acquire, hold, construct, improve, maintain, operate, own, and lease an expressway system.
Qualifications: The governor shall appoint 5 of the 13 members. All members shall be residents of the county. Members appointed by the governor shall not hold an elective office.

Mid-Bay Bridge Authority, Okaloosa County

Authority: Chapter 00-411, Laws of Florida
Term: 3 years
Confirmation Required: None
Oversight: County Jurisdiction
Compensation: Per diem, in accordance with Section 112.061 of the Florida Statutes
Description: A special district authority is created for the purpose of planning for, constructing, operating, and maintaining a bridge transversing Choctawhatchee Bay.
Qualifications: Five members shall be appointed by the governor for a 3 year term; terms shall end June 30. The chairperson and officers are appointed by the authority. No person who has transacted business with the authority is eligible for appointment for a period of 3 years following the transactiion.

Orlando-Orange County Expressway Authority

Authority: Section 348.753, Florida Statutes
Term: 4 years
Confirmation Required: None
Oversight: County Jurisdiction
Compensation: Per diem, in accordance with Section 112.061 of the Florida Statutes
Description: The authority has the right to acquire, hold, construct, improve, maintain, operate, own, and lease in the capacity of lessor, the Orlando–Orange County Expressway System.
Qualifications: Each appointee shall be a person of outstanding reputation in the areas of integrity, responsibility, and business

ability. An appointee may not be an employee of Orange County or any city municipality therein. Three members shall be appointed by the governor.

Port Saint Joe Port Authority, Gulf County

Authority: Chapter 55-30787, Laws of Florida
Term: 4 years
Confirmation Required: None
Oversight: County Jurisdiction
Compensation: Per diem, in accordance with Section 112.061 of the Florida Statutes
Description: The authority is a public agency for the development of the port and commerce, and acquires, maintains, and operates all harbor and port facilities. The authority may also contract or lease port facilities.
Qualifications: No commissioner shall be an officer of the city, county or state. No more than 2 members shall be primarily engaged in the maritime business. Members shall be property owners.

Santa Rosa Bay Bridge Authority

Authority: Chapter 348 Part IX, Florida Statutes
Term: 2 years
Confirmation Required: None
Oversight: County Jurisdiction
Compensation: Per diem, in accordance with Section 112.061 of the Florida Statutes
Description: The authority is responsible for construction of the Santa Rosa County Bay Bridge System, including land purchase and finance agreement, after approval by a resource planning and management committee.
Qualifications: The governor shall appoint 3 of the 7 members. All members shall be permanent residents of Santa Rosa County; none shall be elected officials at the time of appointment. The county commission shall appoint 3 members and the district engineer shall serve as an ex-officio member.

Sarasota-Manatee Airport Authority

Authority: Chapter 00480, Laws of Florida
Term: Pleasure of the Governor
Confirmation Required: None
Oversight: County Jurisdiction
Compensation: Per diem, in accordance with Section 112.061 of the Florida Statutes
Description: Members maintain and operate any airport facility in both the counties of Manatee and Sarasota.
Qualifications: Members shall be appointed by the governor. No member shall serve more than 8 consecutive years. Members shall assume office on the third Tuesday of November.

Southern States Energy Board

Authority: Section 377.711, Florida Statutes
Term: Pleasure of the Governor
Confirmation Required: None
Oversight: Office of the governor
Compensation: Per diem, in accordance with Section 112.061 of the Florida Statutes
Description: The board is the agency by which the member southern states analyze the position of the South, with respect to energy, energy related industries, and environmental concerns.
Qualifications: The board shall be composed of 3 members from each party state, 1 of whom shall be appointed or designated in each state to represent the governor, the state senate, and the state house of representatives, respectively. Each member shall be designated or appointed in accordance with the law of the state which he or she represents and shall serve and be subject to removal in accordance with such law.

St. Lucie County Expressway and Bridge Authority

Authority: Section 348.942, Florida Statutes
Term: 4 years
Confirmation Required: None

Oversight: County Jurisdiction
Compensation: Per diem, in accordance with Section 112.061 of the Florida Statutes
Description: The authority shall exercises control over any expressway system within St. Lucie County and has the right to construct any extensions, additions, or improvements to the system.
Qualifications: Three members shall be appointed by the governor. Initially, 1 member shall be appointed for 2 years; thereafter, all members shall be appointed for 4 year. No member shall be an officer or employee of any city of St. Lucie County.

Tampa Bay Commuter Rail Authority

Authority: Section 343.73, Florida Statutes
Term: 4 years
Confirmation Required: None
Oversight: Department of Transportation
Compensation: Per diem, in accordance with Section 112.061 of the Florida Statutes
Description: The authority establishes and determines policies necessary for the operation and promotion of a commuter rail system and commuter ferry system in the Tampa Bay area of Hernando, Hillsborough, Pasco, Pinellas and Polk Counties.
Qualifications: The governor shall appoint 1 of the 17 members. The metropolitan planning organizations and the county commissions of Hernando, Hillsborough, Pasco, Pinellas and Polk Counties shall each appoint 1 member from their respective county. The secretary of the Department of Transportation shall also appoint 1 member. The local transit authority in each of the above 5 counties shall elect 1 member.

Tampa Port Authority

Authority: Chapter 91-380, Laws of Florida
Term: 4 years
Confirmation Required: Senate
Oversight: County Jurisdiction

Compensation: Per diem, in accordance with Section 112.061 of the Florida Statutes
Description: The authority conducts studies, adopts plans, and carries out the development of the facilities and the traffic through the port. The Tampa Port Authority is the governing body of the Hillsborough County Port District.
Qualifications: Members shall be qualified electors of Hillsborough County with an outstanding reputation for integrity, responsibility, and business ability. No public officer or employee shall serve.

Tampa–Hillsborough County Expressway Authority

Authority: Section 348.52(2), Florida Statutes
Term: 4 years
Confirmation Required: Senate
Oversight: County Jurisdiction
Compensation: Per diem, in accordance with Section 112.061 of the Florida Statutes
Description: The authority promulgates rules and regulations for the use and occupancy of the expressway system, as well as determining routes and the design and type of constructions of the expressway system.
Qualifications: Four members shall be appointed by the governor. Members shall subscribe to an oath of office.

Transportation Outreach Program (TOP) Advisory Council

Authority: Section 339.1378(8), Florida Statutes
Term: 2 years
Confirmation Required: None
Oversight: Department of Transportation
Compensation: Per diem, in accordance with Section 112.061 of the Florida Statutes
Description: The council makes recommendations on: funding transportation projects of a high priority based on the prevailing

principles of preserving the existing transportation infrastructure, enhancing Florida's economic growth and competitiveness, and improving travel choices to ensure mobility.
Qualifications: The council shall consist of 7 members, 3 appointed by the governor. The president of the senate and the Speaker of the House shall each appoint 2 members.

Tri-County Commuter Rail Authority

Authority: Section 343.53, Florida Statutes
Term: 4 years
Confirmation Required: None
Oversight: Department of Transportation
Compensation: Per diem, in accordance with Section 112.061 of the Florida Statutes
Description: The authority establishes and determines policies, as is deemed necessary, for the operation and promotion of a commuter rail system. It also adopts rules, as is deemed necessary, to govern the operation of a commuter rail system and commuter rail facilities.
Qualifications: The authority shall consist of 9 members, 1 appointed by the governor. The county commission of Dade, Broward, and Palm Beach Counties shall each appoint 1 commissioner and 1 layperson from their respective counties. The secretary of transportation shall appoint 1 member. The remaining members shall appoint 1 additional member. Terms shall be staggered.

West Orange Airport Authority

Authority: Chapter 99-482, Laws of Florida
Term: 4 years
Confirmation Required: None
Oversight: County Jurisdiction
Compensation: Per diem, in accordance with Section 112.061 of the Florida Statutes

Description: The authority is created for the purpose of performing such acts, as is deemed necessary for the sound planning, development, and management of an airport, which shall include industry, commerce, and business.

Qualifications: The authority shall consist of 9 members, 3 appointed by the governor. Each member shall be a resident and elector of the state.

Governor's Executive Office Staff

In addition to boards, commissions, cabinet secretaries, agency heads and other executive level appointments, the governor appoints several high profile staff positions. A sampling of the duties and responsibilities of these staff positions is included below:

- The *Chief of Staff* and 3 *Deputy Chiefs of Staff* assist the governor in the creation and implementation of policies through legislation, the budgetary process, and supervision of state agencies.
- The *Director of Cabinet Affairs* assists the governor in carrying out his or her duties with the cabinet and also serves as liaison with cabinet departments and agencies.
- The *Director of Citizens Services* oversees 2 units: the correspondence unit, which ensures responses to all correspondence for the governor, and the citizens' assistance unit, which monitors agencies under the governor's direct jurisdiction.
- The *Communications Director* assists the governor with the dissemination of information regarding the governor's programs and initiatives.

- The *Press Secretary* provides information to radio, print and television journalists, issues press releases, schedules press conferences, and announces appointments to various offices.
- The *Appointments Director* supports the governor in appointing qualified representatives and appropriate people to a large number of important leadership roles throughout the state.
- The *Director of External Affairs* supports the governor's public appearances by advancing his or her schedule, coordinates volunteer and community initiatives around the state, and acts as liaison for the governor with various public service groups.
- The *Legal Affairs General Counsel* functions as the legal counsel or adviser to the governor in his or her official capacity. Legal office personnel also serve as liaisons in other areas of the state.
- The *Director of Legislative Affairs* provides counsel and support to the governor and other staff members with regard to legislative matters and concerns. He or she advocates for, and helps secure the passage of the governor's legislative priorities.
- The *Director of Administration* handles all personnel, purchasing, and support issues for the governor and his or her staff.
- The *Director of Florida's Washington Office* serves as the state's federal relations representative in Washington D.C., monitoring legislation and coordinating the efforts of Florida's congressional delegation.
- The *Director of Scheduling* handles the day-to-day schedule for the office of the governor, responds to requests for public appearances, and advances the governor's schedule to the appropriate entities.

- The *Director of the Office of Information Systems* has responsibilities for computer support within the governor's office, in order to enhance the efficiency and effectiveness of office operations.
- The *Director of the Office of Policy and Budget,* along with *2 Deputy Directors,* provide coordinated planning, policy development, budgeting, and evaluation for the governor with the governor's priorities in mind.
- The *Chief Inspector General* is responsible for promoting accountability, integrity, and efficiency in the governor's executive office, as well as in the agencies under the governor's jurisdiction.

Sample Copy Only

QUESTIONNAIRE
for
GUBERNATORIAL APPOINTMENTS

Appendix 1

THE FLORIDA GUIDE TO POLITICAL APPOINTMENTS

FOR THE GOVERNOR'S APPOINTMENT OFFICE
The Capitol, Tallahassee, Florida 32399-0001

The information from this page has been requested and will be used exclusively by the GOVERNOR'S OFFICE. **Please type or use black ink.**

1. Board of Interest: _____

2. Current Employer and Occupation: _____

3. Are you applying for reappointment?   Yes ☐   No ☐

4. *Do you have a disability?   Yes ☐   No ☐   If "Yes", please describe your disability that would qualify you for this appointment, if applicable.

5. *Sex: Male ☐   Female ☐

6. *Race: White ☐   Native-American/Alaskan Native ☐
           Hispanic-American ☐   Asian/Pacific Islander ☐
           African-American ☐

7. Do you now, or have you, within the last three years, been a member of any club or organization that, to your knowledge, in practice or policy, restricts membership or restricted membership during the time that you belonged on the basis of race, religion, national origin, or gender? If so, detail the name and nature of the club(s) or organization(s), relevant policies and practices, and state whether you intend to continue as a member if you appointed by the Governor.

8. One of the Governor's top priorities is to improve the conditions of the children living in our state. Would you be willing to spend an hour a week with a child in need in your community? If so, please identify the type of program and/or activity you would be willing to participate in as a mentor.

_____
Applicant's Name, including name
commonly used (Please print)

* This information will be used to provide demographic statistics and is not requested for the purpose of discriminating on any basis.

Revised 6/2000

ELIZABETH MCCALLUM

QUESTIONNAIRE FOR GUBERNATORIAL APPOINTMENTS

The information from this questionnaire will be used by the Governor's office and, where applicable, The Florida Senate in considering action on your confirmation. The questionnaire <u>MUST BE COMPLETED IN FULL.</u> Answer "none" or "not applicable" where appropriate. **Please type or print in black ink.**

Date Completed _____

1. Name: _____
   MR./MRS./MS.   LAST   FIRST   MIDDLE/MAIDEN

2. Business Address: _____
                     STREET   OFFICE #   CITY

   _____
   POST OFFICE BOX   STATE   ZIP CODE   AREA CODE/PHONE NUMBER

3. Residence Address: _____
                      STREET   CITY   COUNTY

   _____
   POST OFFICE BOX   STATE   ZIP CODE   AREA CODE/PHONE NUMBER

   Specify the preferred mailing address: Business ☐   Residence ☐   Fax # _____
                                                                        (optional)

4. A. List all your places of residence for the last five (5) years.

   ADDRESS   CITY & STATE   FROM   TO
   _____
   _____
   _____
   _____

   B. List all your former and current residences outside of Florida that you have maintained at any time during adulthood.

   ADDRESS   CITY & STATE   FROM   TO
   _____
   _____
   _____

5. Date of Birth: _____   Place of Birth: _____
6. Social Security Number: _____
7. Driver License Number: _____   Issuing State: _____
8. Have you ever used or been known by any other legal name? Yes ☐ No ☐ If "Yes" Explain
   _____
   _____
   _____

Revised 6/2000

THE FLORIDA GUIDE TO POLITICAL APPOINTMENTS

9. Are you a United States citizen? Yes ☐ No ☐ If "No" explain: _____
   _____
   _____
   _____

   If you are a naturalized citizen, date of naturalization: _____
10. Since what year have you been a continuous resident of Florida? _____
11. Are you a registered Florida voter? Yes ☐ No ☐ If "Yes" list:
    A. County of registration: _____ B. Current party affiliation: _____
12. Education
    A. High School: _____ Year Graduated: _____
              (NAME AND LOCATION)

    B. List all postsecondary educational institutions attended:

NAME & LOCATION	DATES ATTENDED	CERTIFICATES/DEGREES RECEIVED

13. Are you or have you ever been a member of the armed forces of the United States? Yes ☐ No ☐ If "Yes" list:
    A. Dates of service: _____
    B. Branch or component: _____
    C. Date & type of discharge: _____
14. Have you ever been arrested, charged, or indicted for violation of any federal, state, county, or municipal law, regulation, or ordinance? (Exclude traffic violations for which a fine or civil penalty of $150 or less was paid.) If "Yes" give details:

DATE	PLACE	NATURE	DISPOSITION

15. Concerning your current employer and for all of your employment during the last five years, list your employer's name, business address, type of business, occupation or job title, and period(s) of employment.

EMPLOYER'S NAME & ADDRESS	TYPE OF BUSINESS	OCCUPATION/JOB TITLE	PERIOD OF EMPLOYMENT

16. Have you ever been employed by any state, district, or local governmental agency in Florida? Yes ☐ No ☐
    If "Yes", identify the position(s), the name(s) of the employing agency, and the period(s) of employment:

POSITION	EMPLOYING AGENCY	PERIOD OF EMPLOYMENT

Revised 6/2000

3

17. A. State your experiences and interests or elements of your personal history that qualify you for this appointment.

_____
_____
_____
_____
_____
_____

B. Have you received any degree(s), professional certification(s), or designations(s) related to the subject matter of this appointment? Yes ☐   No ☐   If "Yes", list:

_____
_____
_____

C. Have you received any awards or recognitions relating to the subject matter of this appointment? Yes ☐   No ☐ If "Yes", list:

_____
_____
_____

D. Identify all association memberships and association offices held by you that relate to this appointment:

_____
_____
_____
_____
_____

18. Do you currently hold an office or position (appointive, civil service, or other) with the federal or any foreign government? Yes ☐   No ☐   If "Yes", list:

_____
_____
_____
_____

19. A. Have you ever been elected or appointed to any public office in this state?   Yes ☐   No ☐   If "Yes", state the office title, date of election or appointment, term of office, and level of government (city, county, district, state, federal):

OFFICE TITLE	DATE OF ELECTION OR APPOINTMENT	TERM OF OFFICE	LEVEL OF GOVERNMENT

Revised 6/2000

B. If your service was on an appointed board(s), committee(s), or council(s):

   (1) How frequently were meetings scheduled: _____

   (2) If you missed any of the regularly scheduled meetings, state the number of meetings you attended, the number you missed, and the reasons(s) for your absence(s).

MEETINGS ATTENDED	MEETINGS MISSED	REASON FOR ABSENCE

20. Has probable cause ever been found that you were in violation of Part III, Chapter 112, F.S., the Code of Ethics for Public Officers and Employees? Yes ☐ No ☐ If "Yes", give details:

DATE	NATURE OF VIOLATION	DISPOSITION

21. Have you ever been suspended from any office by the Governor of the State of Florida? Yes ☐ No ☐ If "Yes", list:

   A. Title of office: _____ C. Reason for suspension: _____

   B. Date of suspension: _____ D. Result: Reinstated ☐ Removed ☐ Resigned ☐

22. Have you previously been appointed to any office that required confirmation by the Florida Senate? Yes ☐ No ☐ If "Yes", list:

   A. Title of Office: _____

   B. Term of Appointment: _____

   C. Confirmation results: _____

23. Have you ever been refused a fidelity, surety, performance, or other bond? Yes ☐ No ☐ If "Yes", explain: _____

24. Have you held or do you hold an occupational or professional license or certificate in the State of Florida? Yes ☐ No ☐ If "Yes", provide the title and number, original issue date, and issuing authority. If any disciplinary action (fine, probation, suspension, revocation, disbarment) has ever been taken against you by the issuing authority, state the type and date of the action taken:

LICENSE/CERTIFICATE TITLE & NUMBER	ORIGINAL ISSUE DATE	ISSUING AUTHORITY	DISCIPLINARY ACTION/DATE

25. A. Have you, or businesses of which you have been and owner, officer, or employee, held any contractual or other direct dealings during the last four (4) years with any state or local governmental agency in Florida, including the office or agency to which you have been appointed or are seeking appointment? Yes ☐ No ☐ If "Yes", explain:

NAME OF BUSINESS	YOUR RELATIONSHIP TO BUSINESS	BUSINESS' RELATIONSHIP TO AGENCY

Revised 6/2000

ELIZABETH MCCALLUM

B. Have members of your immediate family (spouse, child, parents(s), siblings(s)), or businesses of which members of your immediate family have been owners, officers, or employees, held any contractual or other direct dealings during the last four (4) years with any state or local governmental agency in Florida, including the office or agency to which you have been appointed or are seeking appointment? Yes ☐ No ☐ If "Yes", explain:

NAME OF BUSINESS	FAMILY MEMBER'S RELATIONSHIP TO YOU	FAMILY MEMBER'S RELATIONSHIP TO BUSINESS	BUSINESS' RELATIONSHIP TO AGENCY

26. Have you ever been a registered lobbyist or have you lobbied at any level of government at any time during the past five (5) years? Yes ☐ No ☐

   A. Did you receive any compensation other than reimbursement for expenses? Yes ☐ No ☐

   B. Name of agency or entity you lobbied and the principal(s) you represented:

AGENCY LOBBIED	PRINCIPAL REPRESENTED

27. List three persons who have known you well within the past five (5) years. Include a current, complete address and telephone number. Exclude your relatives and members of the Florida Senate.

NAME	MAILING ADDRESS	ZIP CODE	AREA CODE/PHONE NUMBER

28. Name any business, professional, occupational, civic, or fraternal organizations(s) of which you are now a member, or of which you have been a member during the past five (5) years, the organization address(es), and date(s) of your membership(s).

NAME	MAILING ADDRESS	OFFICE(S) HELD & TERM	DATE(S) OF MEMBERSHIP

29. Do you know of any reason why you will not be able to attend fully to the duties of the office or position to which you have been or will be appointed? Yes ☐ No ☐ If "Yes", explain:

30. If required by law or administrative rule, will you file financial disclosure statements? Yes ☐ No ☐

Revised 6/2000

CERTIFICATION

STATE OF FLORIDA, COUNTY OF

Before me, the undersigned Notary Public of Florida, personally appeared _____, who, after being duly sworn, say: (1) that he/she has carefully and personally prepared or read the answers to the foregoing questions; (2) that the information contained in said answers is complete and true; and (3) that he/she will, as an appointee, fully support the Constitutions of the United States and of the State of Florida.

_____
Signature of Applicant-Affiant

Sworn to and subscribed before me
this_____ day of _____, 20___.

_____
Signature of Notary Public-State of Florida

_____
(Print, Type, or Stamp Commissioned Name of Notary Public)

My commission expires: _____

Personally Known ☐ OR Produced Identification ☐
Type of Identification Produced _____

(seal)

Revised 6/2000

Sample Copy

Judicial Appointment Application Form

created by the Judicial Nominating Commission

Appendix 2

THE FLORIDA GUIDE TO POLITICAL APPOINTMENTS

APPLICATION FOR NOMINATION TO THE _____ COURT
(Please attach additional pages as needed to respond fully to questions.)

DATE: _____ Florida Bar No.: _____

GENERAL: Soc. Sec. No.: _____

1. Name _____ E-mail: _____

   Date Admitted to Practice in Florida: _____

2. State title currently held; including professional position and any public or judicial office.

3. Business address: _____

   City _____ State _____ ZIP _____

   Telephone _____ FAX _____

4. Residential address: _____

   City _____ State _____ ZIP _____

   Since _____ Telephone _____

5. Place of birth: _____

   Date of birth: _____ Age _____

6. Length of residence in State of Florida _____

7. Marital status _____

   If married: _____

   Spouse's name _____

   Date of marriage _____

   Spouse's occupation _____

   If ever divorced give for each marriage name(s) of spouse(s), current address for each former spouse, date and place of divorce.

Page 1

ELIZABETH MCCALLUM

8. Children

    Name(s)   *Ages(s)*   *Occupation(s)*   *Residential address(es)*

9. Military Service (including Reserves)

    Service   *Branch*   *Highest Rank*   *Dates*

Rank at time of discharge   Type of discharge

Awards or citations

HEALTH:

10. Are you currently addicted to or dependent upon the use of narcotics, drugs, or intoxicating beverages? If yes, state the details, including the date.

11a. During the last ten years have you been hospitalized or have you consulted a professional or have you received treatment or a diagnosis from a professional for any of the following: Kleptomania, Pathological or Compulsive Gambling, Pedophilia, Exhibitionism or Voyeurism?

    Yes ☐   No ☐

If your answer is yes, please direct each such professional, hospital and other facility to furnish the Chairperson of the Commission any information the Commission may request with respect to any such hospitalization, consultation, treatment or diagnosis. ["Professional" includes a Physician, Psychiatrist, Psychologist, Psychotherapist or Mental Health Counselor.]

Please describe such treatment or diagnosis.

Page 2

11b. In the past ten years have any of the following occurred to you which would interfere with your ability to work in a competent and professional manner?

- Experiencing periods of no sleep for 2 or 3 nights
- Experiencing periods of hyperactivity
- Spending money profusely with extremely poor judgment
- Suffered from extreme loss of appetite
- Issuing checks without sufficient funds
- Defaulting on a loan
- Experiencing frequent mood swings
- Uncontrollable tiredness
- Falling asleep without warning in the middle of an activity

Yes ☐   No ☐

If yes, please explain.

12a. Do you currently have a physical or mental impairment which in any way limits, your ability or fitness to properly exercise your duties as a member of the Judiciary in a competent and professional manner?

Yes ☐   No ☐

12b. If your answer to the question above is Yes, are the limitations or impairments caused by your physical or mental health impairment reduced or ameliorated because you receive ongoing treatment (with or without medication) or participate in a monitoring or counseling program?

Yes ☐   No ☐

Describe such problem and any treatment or program of monitoring or counseling.

13. During the last ten years, have you ever been declared legally incompetent or have you or your property been placed under any guardianship, conservatorship or committee? If yes, give full details as to court, date and circumstances.

14. During the last ten years, have you unlawfully used controlled substances, narcotic drugs or dangerous drugs as defined by Federal or State laws? If your answer is "Yes," explain in detail. (Unlawful use includes the use of one or more drugs and/or the unlawful possession or distribution of drugs. It does not include the use of drugs taken under supervision of a licensed health care professional or other uses authorized by Federal law provisions.)

15. In the past year, have you ever been reprimanded, demoted, disciplined, placed on probation, suspended, cautioned or terminated by an employer as result of your alleged consumption of alcohol, prescription drugs or illegal use of drugs? If so, please state the circumstances under which such action was taken, the name(s) of any persons who took such action, and the background and resolution of such action.

Page 3

16. Within the last five years, have you ever been formally reprimanded, demoted, disciplined, cautioned, placed on probation, suspended or terminated by an employer? If so, please state the circumstances under which such action was taken, the date(s) such action was taken, the name(s) of any persons who took such action, and the background and resolution of such action.

17. Have any of your current or former co-workers, subordinates, supervisors, customers or clients ever filed a formal complaint or accusation of misconduct against you with any regulatory or investigatory agency, or with your employer? If so, please state the date(s) of such formal accusation(s), and the specific formal accusation(s) made, and the background and resolution of such action(s).

18. Have you ever refused to submit to a test to determine whether you had consumed and/or were under the influence of alcohol or drugs? If so, please state the date you were requested to submit to such a test, type of test required, the name of the entity requesting that you submit to the test, the outcome of your refusal and the reason why you refused to submit to such a test.

19. In the past year, have you failed to meet any deadline imposed by court order or received notice that you have not complied with substantive requirements of any business or contractual arrangement? If so, please explain in full.

20. In the past ten years, have you suffered memory loss or impaired judgment for any reason? If so, please explain in full.

21. Are you currently the subject of an investigation which could result in civil, administrative or criminal action against you? If yes, please state the nature of the investigation, the agency conducting the investigation and the expected completion date of the investigation.

22. In the past ten years, have you been subject to or threatened with eviction proceedings? If yes, please explain.

EDUCATION:

23a. Secondary schools, colleges and law schools attended.

Schools	Class Standing	Dates of Attendance	Degree

23b. List and describe academic scholarships earned, honor societies or other awards.

THE FLORIDA GUIDE TO POLITICAL APPOINTMENTS

NON-LEGAL EMPLOYMENT:

24. List *all* previous full-time non-legal jobs or positions held since 21 in chronological order and briefly describe them.

Date	Position	Employer	Address

PROFESSIONAL ADMISSIONS:

25. List all courts (including state bar admissions) and administrative bodies having special admission requirements to which you are presently admitted to practice, giving the dates of admission.

Court or Administrative Body	Date of Admission

LAW PRACTICE: (If you are a sitting judge, answer this series of questions with reference to the years before you became a judge.)

26. State the names, dates and addresses for all firms with which you have been associated in practice, governmental agencies or private business organizations by which you have been employed, periods you have practiced as a sole practitioner, law clerkships and other prior employment:

Position	Name of Firm	Address	Dates

27. Describe the general nature of your current practice including any designated areas of practice or certifications which you possess; additionally, if your practice is substantially different from your prior practice or if you are not now practicing law, give details of prior practice. Describe your typical clients or former clients and the problems for which they sought your services.

28a. What percentage of your appearance in courts in the last five years was in:

ELIZABETH MCCALLUM

Federal Court?	%	State County Court?		%
State Circuit Court		Administrative Bodies?		%
(General)?	%	Criminal Court?		%
Probate Court?	%	Juvenile Court?		%
Appellate Court?	%	General Master Hearings?		%

28b. For your last five cases, which were either contested or tried, list the names and telephone numbers of trial counsel on either side.

29a. During the last five years, what percentage of your practice has been trial practice?   %

29b. How frequently have you appeared at administrative hearings?   times per month

29c. How frequently have you appeared in Court?   times per month

29d. What percentage of your practice involving litigation has been civil?   %

29e. What percentage of your practice involving litigation has been criminal?   %

29f. If your practice was substantially personal injury, what percentage of your work was in representation of plaintiffs?   % defendants?   %

29g. How many (number) of the cases you have tried to verdict or judgment were:

    Jury?   Non-jury?

    Arbitration?   Administrative Bodies?

29h. For the cases you have tried to conclusion in arbitration, before administrative bodies or in courts of record during each of the past five years, indicate whether you were sole, associate or chief counsel. Give citations of any reported cases.

29i. List and describe the five most significant cases which you personally litigated giving case style, number and citation to reported decisions, if any. Identify your client and describe the nature of your participation in the case and the reason you believe it to be significant. Give the name of the court and judge, the date tried and names of other attorneys involved.

29j. Attach at least one example of legal writing which you personally wrote. If you have not personally written any legal documents recently, you may attach writing for which you had substantial responsibility. Please describe your degree of involvement in preparing the writing you attach.

30. If during any prior period you have appeared in court with greater frequency than during the last five years, indicate the period during which this was so and give for such prior periods a succinct statement of the part you played in the litigation, numbers of cases and whether jury or non-jury.

PRIOR JUDICIAL EXPERIENCE OR PUBLIC OFFICE:

Page 6

31a. Have you ever held judicial office or been a candidate for judicial office? If so, state the court(s) involved and the dates of service or dates of candidacy.

31b. List any prior quasi-judicial service:

      Dates   Name of Agency   Position Held

    Types of issues heard:

31c. Have you ever held or been a candidate for any other public office? If so, state the office, location and dates of service or candidacy.

31d. If you have had prior judicial or quasi-judicial experience,

    (i)   List the names, phone numbers and addresses of six attorneys who appeared before you on matters of substance.

    (ii)   Describe the approximate number and nature of the cases you have handled during your judicial or quasi-judicial tenure.

    (iii)   List citations of any opinions which have been published.

    (iv)   List citations or styles and describe the five most significant cases you have tried or heard. Identify the parties, describe the cases and tell why you believe them to be significant. Give dates tried and names of attorneys involved.

    (v)   Has a complaint about you ever been made to the Judicial Qualifications Commission? If so, give date, describe complaint and its resolution.

    (vi)   Have you ever held an attorney in contempt? If so, for each instance state name of attorney, approximate date and circumstances.

BUSINESS INVOLVEMENT:

32a. If you are now an officer, director or otherwise engaged in the management of any business enterprise, state the name of such enterprise, the nature of the business, the nature of your duties, and whether you intend to resign such position immediately upon your appointment or election to judicial office.

32b. Since being admitted to the Bar, have you ever been engaged in any occupation, business or profession other than the practice of law? If so, give details, including dates.

32c. State whether during the past five years you have received any fees or compensation of any kind, other than for legal services rendered, from any business enterprise, institution, organization, or association of any kind. If so, identify the source of such compensation, the nature of the business enterprise, institution, organization or association involved and the dates such compensation was paid and the amounts.

POSSIBLE BIAS OR PREJUDICE:

33. The Commission is interested in knowing if there are certain types of cases, groups of entities, or extended relationships or associations which would limit the cases for which you could sit as the presiding judge. Please list all types or classifications of cases or litigants for which you as a general proposition believe it would be difficult for you to sit as the presiding judge. Indicate the reason for each situation as to why you believe you might be in conflict. If you have prior judicial experience, describe the types of cases from which you have recused yourself.

MISCELLANEOUS:

34. Have you ever been convicted for violation of any federal, state, county or municipal law, regulation or ordinance? If so, give details. Do not include traffic violations for which a fine of $100 or less was imposed unless it also included a jail sentence.

35a. Have you ever been sued by a client? If so, give particulars including name of client, date suit filed, court, case number and disposition.

35b. Have you or your professional liability insurance carrier ever settled a claim against you for professional malpractice? If so, give particulars, including the amounts involved.

36a. Have you ever filed a personal petition in bankruptcy or has a petition in bankruptcy been filed against you?

36b. Have you ever owned more than 20% of the issued and outstanding shares or acted as an officer or director of any corporation by which or against which a petition in bankruptcy has been filed? If so, give name of corporation, your relationship to it and date and caption of petition.

37. Have you ever been a party to a lawsuit either as a plaintiff or as a defendant? If so, please supply style, case number, nature of the lawsuit, whether you were Plaintiff or Defendant and its disposition.

38. Has there ever been a finding of probable cause or other citation issued against you or are you presently under investigation for a breach of ethics or unprofessional conduct by any court, administrative agency, bar association, or other professional group. If so, give the particulars.

39a. Have you filed all past tax returns as required by federal, state, local and other government authorities?

Yes ☐ No ☐ If no, explain.

39b. Have you ever paid a tax penalty?

Yes ☐ No ☐ If yes, explain what and why.

39c. Has a tax lien ever been filed against you? If so, by whom, when, where and why?

HONORS AND PUBLICATIONS:

40. If you have published any books or articles, list them, giving citations and dates.

41. List any honors, prizes or awards you have received. Give dates.

42. List and describe any speeches or lectures you have given.

PROFESSIONAL AND OTHER ACTIVITIES:

43a. List all bar associations and professional societies of which you are a member and give the titles and dates of any office which you may have held in such groups and committees to which you belonged.

43b. List, in a fully identifiable fashion, all organizations other than those identified in response to question No. 43(a), of which you have been a member since graduating from law school, including the titles and dates of any offices which you have held in each such organization.

43c. List your hobbies or other vocational interests.

43d. Do you now or have you ever belonged to any club or organization that in practice or policy restricts (or restricted during the time of your membership) its membership on the basis of race, religion, national origin or sex? If so, detail the name and nature of the club(s) or organization(s), relevant policies and practices and whether you intend to continue as a member if you are selected to serve on the bench.

43e. Describe any pro bono legal work you have done. Give dates.

SUPPLEMENTAL INFORMATION:

44a. Have you attended any continuing legal education programs during the past five years? If so, in what substantive areas?

44b. Have you taught any courses on law or lectured at bar association conferences, law school forums, or continuing legal education programs? If so, in what substantive areas?

45. Describe any additional education or other experience you have which could assist you in holding judicial office.

46. Explain the particular potential contribution you believe your selection would bring to this position.

47. If you have previously submitted a questionnaire or application to this or any other judicial nominating commission, please give the name of the commission and the approximate date of submission.

48. Give any other information you feel would be helpful to the Commission in evaluating your application.

REFERENCES:

49. List the names, addresses and telephone numbers of ten persons who are in a position to comment on your qualifications for judicial position and of whom inquiry may be made by the Commission.

CERTIFICATE

I have read the foregoing questions carefully and have answered them truthfully, fully and completely. I hereby waive notice by and authorize The Florida Bar or any of its committees, educational and other institutions, the Judicial Qualifications Commission, the Florida Board of Bar Examiners or any judicial or professional disciplinary or supervisory body or commission, any references furnished by me, employers, business and professional associates, all governmental agencies and instrumentalities and all consumer and credit reporting agencies to release to the respective Judicial Nominating Commission and Office of the Governor any information, files, records or credit reports requested by the commission in connection with any consideration of me as possible nominee for appointment to judicial office. Information relating to any Florida Bar disciplinary proceedings is to be made available in accordance with Rule 3-7.1(q)(2), Rules Regulating The Florida Bar. I recognize and agree that, pursuant to the Florida Constitution and the Uniform Rules of this commission, the contents of this questionnaire and other information received from or concerning me, and all interviews and proceedings of the commission, except for deliberations by the commission, shall be open to the public.

Dated this _____ day of _____, 20____.

_____
Signature

Pursuant to Section 119.07(k)1, F.S., . . . The home addresses and telephone numbers of justices of the Supreme Court, district court of appeal judges, circuit court judges, and county court judges; the home addresses, telephone numbers, and places of employment of the spouses and children of justices and judges; and the names and locations of schools and day care facilities attended by the children of justices and judges are exempt from the provisions of subsection (1), dealing with public records.

Page 11

ELIZABETH MCCALLUM

FINANCIAL HISTORY

In lieu of answering the questions on this page, you may attach copies of your completed Federal Income Tax Returns for the preceding three (3) years. Those income tax returns should include returns from a professional association. If you answer the questions on this page, you do not have to file copies of your tax returns.

1. State the amount of gross income you have earned, or losses you have incurred (before deducting expenses and taxes) from the practice of law for the preceding three-year period. This income figure should include salary, if the nature of your employment is in a legal field.

2. State the amount of net income you have earned, or losses you have incurred (after deducting expenses but not taxes) from the practice of law for the preceding three-year period. This income figure should include salary, if the nature of your employment is in a legal field.

3. State the gross amount of income or losses incurred (before deducting expenses or taxes) you have earned in the preceding three years from all sources other than the practice of law, and generally describe the source of such income or losses.

4. State the amount of net income you have earned or losses incurred (after deducting expenses) from sources other than the practice of law for the preceding three-year period, and generally describe the sources of such income or losses.

JUDICIAL APPLICATION DATE RECORD

> The judicial application shall include a separate page asking applicants to identify their race, ethnicity and gender. Completion of this page shall be optional, and the page shall include an explanation that the information is requested for date collection purposes in order to assess and promote diversity in the judiciary. The chair of the Commission shall forward all such completed pages, along with the names of the nominees to the JNC Coordinator at The Florida Bar (pursuant to JNC Uniform Rule of Procedure)

(Please Type or Print)

Date: _____

JNC Submitting To: _____

Name (please print): _____
Current Occupation: _____
Telephone Number: _____ Attorney No.: _____
Gender (check one): ☐ Male   ☐ Female
Ethnic Origin (check one):
  ☐ White, non Hispanic
  ☐ Hispanic
  ☐ Black
  ☐ American Indian/Alaskan Native
  ☐ Asian/Pacific Islander

County of Residence: _____

Index

– A –

Acquisition and Restoration Council, 30
Adjutant General of the Department of Military Affairs, 154
Affordable Housing Study Commission, 140
Alligator Point Water Resources Board, 30
Alzheimer's Disease Advisory Committee, 108
Americans with Disabilities Act Working Group, 140
Annual Report on Graduate Medical Education Committee, 108
Apalachicola-Chattahoochee-Flint River Basin Commission, 31
Appellate District Judicial Nominating Commissions, 87
Appointments Director, 188
Atlantic States Marine Fisheries Commission, 31

– B –

Baker County Hospital Authority, 109
Baker County Development Commission, 154
Barbers Board, 56
Battered Woman Syndrome Panels, 76
Biomedical Research Advisory Council, 109
Board of Accountancy, 56
Board of Acupuncture, 110
Board of Architecture and Interior Design, 57
Board of Athletic Training, 110
Board of Auctioneers, 57
Board of Chiropractic Medicine, 111
Board of Clinical Laboratory Personnel, 111
Board of Clinical Social Work, Marriage, and Family Therapy, 112
Board of Commissioners, Halifax Hospital Medical Center, 112
Board of Commissioners, North Broward Hospital District, 113
Board of Commissioners, South Broward Hospital District, 113
Board of Control for Southern Regional Education, 92
Board of Cosmetology, 58
Board of Dentistry, 113
Board of Directors of the Florida Commercial Space Financing, 168
Board of Directors, Enterprise Florida, Inc., 58
Board of Directors, Florida Alzheimer's Center and Research Institute, 114
Board of Directors, Florida Center for Nursing, 114
Board of Directors, Florida Education Fund, 92
Board of Directors, Florida Fund for Minority Teachers, Inc., 93
Board of Directors, Florida Healthy Kids Corporation, 141
Board of Directors, Florida Sports Foundation, 46
Board of Directors, Workforce Florida, Inc., 59
Board of Employee Leasing Companies, 59
Board of Funeral and Cementery Services, 60
Board of Funeral Directors and Embalmers, 60
Board of Hearing Aid Specialists, 115
Board of Landscape Architecture, 61
Board of Massage Therapy, 115
Board of Medicine, 116
Board of Nursing, 116
Board of Nursing Home Administrators, 117
Board of Occupational Therapy Practice, 117
Board of Opticianry, 118

Board of Optometry, 118
Board of Orthotists and
    Prosthetists, 118
Board of Osteopathic Medicine, 119
Board of Pharmacy, 119
Board of Physical Therapy Practice, 120
Board of Pilot Commissioners, 61
Board of Podiatric Medicine, 120
Board of Professional Engineers, 62
Board of Professional Geologists, 62
Board of Professional Surveyors and
    Mappers, 62
Board of Psychology, 121
Board of Respiratory Care, 121
Board of Speech-Language Pathology and
    Audiology, 122
Board of Supervisors, Florida Space
    Authority, 168
Board of Supervisors, Miami-Date
    County Community Improvement
    Trust, 154
Board of Trustees, Community
    Colleges, 97
Board of Trustees, Florida School for the
    Deaf and the Blind, 93
Board of Trustees, Florida Virtual High
    School, 94
Board of Trustees, Universities, 94
Board of Veterinary Medicine, 63
Boating Advisory Council, 32
Bradford County Development
    Authority, 155

– C –

Campbellton-Graceville Hospital
    Corporation, 122
Cape Canaveral Hospital District, Brevard
    County, 122
Capital Collateral Attorneys, 76
Carrabelle-Franklin Port and Airport
    Authority, 169
Central Florida Regional Transportation
    Authority, 169
Chair of the Emerging Technology
    Commission, 91
Chair of the Florida Arts Council, 46
Chair of the Florida Board of
    Governors, 91
Chair of the Parole Commission, 76

Chair of the Public Employee Relations
    Commission , 56
Chair of the Public Service
    Commission, 168
Chair of the State Board of Education, 91
Chair of the Unemployment Appeals
    Commission , 56
Charter School Review Panel, 95
Chief Inspector General , 189
Chief of Staff, 187
Child Care Executive Partnership, 63
Children's Services Councils , 141
Circuit Courts Judgeship, 86
Civil Service Board of Escambia
    County, 155
Clay County Development Authority, 156
Clay County Utility Authority, 170
College Reach-Out Advisory Council, 95
Commission for Independent
    Education, 96
Commission for the Transportation
    Disadvantaged, 170
Commission on Ethics, 156
Commission on Responsible
    Fatherhood, 142
Commission on the Administration of
    Justice in Capital Cases, 76
Commissioner of Deeds for the State of
    Florida, 56
Commissioner of Education, 91
Committee to Review the State
    Comprehensive Plan, 157
Commuity Hospital Educational
    Council, 123
Communications Director, 187
Construction Industry Licensing
    Board, 64
Continuing Care Advisory Council, 123
Conversion Charter School Pilot Program
    Statewide Selection Panel, 96
Correctional Privatization
    Commission, 77
Council for Education Policy Research
    and Improvement, 97
Council of Economic Advisors, 64
Council on Homelessness, 142
County Courts Judgeship, 86
Courts of Appeal Judgeship, 86

Criminal and Juvenile Justice Information Systems Council, 77
Criminal and Juvenile Justice Standards and Training Commission, 78

– D –

Daytona Beach Racing and Recreational Facilities Commission, 46
Department of Elderly Affairs Advisory Council, 124
Department of Financial Services Committee of Transition Management, 157
Deputy Chief of Staff, 187
Deputy Director for the Office of Policy and Budget, 189
Diabetes Advisory Council, 124
Director of Administration, 188
Director of Cabinet Affairs, 187
Director of Citizen Services, 187
Director of External Affairs, 188
Director of Florida's Washington Office., 188
Director of Legislative Affairs , 188
Director of Scheduling, 188
Director of the Agency for Workforce Innovation, 56
Director of the Govenor's Mansion, 46
Director of the Office of Drug Control Policy, 76
Director of the Office of Information Systems, 189
Director of the office of Long Term Care Policy, 108
Director of the Office of Policy and Budget, 189
Director of the Office of Tourism, Trade and Economic Development, 56
Director of the Office of Urban Opportunity, 140
District Medicdal Examiners, 76
Dr. Martin Luther King, Jr. Commemorative Commission, 47

– E –

Eastpoint Water and Sewer District, 158
Education Commission of the States, 98
Electrical Contractors Licensing Board, 65
Emeral Coast Bridge Authority, 171
Emerging Technology Commission, 98

Environmental Regulation Commission, 32
Escambia County Interstate 110 Extension Authority, 171
Escambia County Utilities Authority, 172
Executive Director of the Department of Citrus, 30
Executive Director of the Department of Highway Safety and Motor Vehicles, 168
Executive Director of the Department of Law Enforcement, 76
Executive Director of the Department of Revenue , 154
Executive Director of the Department of Veteran's Affairs, 140
Executive Director of the Fish and Wildlife Conservation Commission, 30
Executive Director of the State Board of Administration, 154
Executive Director of the State office on Homelessness, 140
Executive Director of the State Technology Office, 154
Executive Director of the Statewide Public Guardianship, 140
Expressway Authority of Broward County, 172

– F –

Family Care Councils, 143
FCAT Blue Ribbon Task Force, 99
Fiesta of Five Flags Commission of Pensacola, 47
Fish and Wildlife Conservation Commission, 33
Florida Arts Council, 48
Florida Black Business Investment Board, 65
Florida Board of Governors, 99
Florida Building Code Administrators and Inspectors Board, 66
Florida Building Commission, 66
Florida Cancer Control and Research Advisory Council, 125
Florida Citrus Commission, 33
Florida Commission of Tourism, 48

Florida Commission on African-American Affairs, 143
Florida Commission on Community Service, 144
Florida Commission on Human Relations, 145
Florida Commission on the Status of Women, 145
Florida Commission on Veterans' Affairs, 146
Florida Communities Trust, 158
Florida Corrections Commission, 78
Florida Crime Laboratory Council, 79
Florida Development Finance Corporation, 66
Florida Developmental Disabilities Council, 125
Florida Elections Commission, 159
Florida Employee Long-Term Care Plan Board of Directors, 126
Florida Endowment Foundation for Vocational Rehabilitation, 100
Florida Film and Entertainment Advisory Council, 49
Florida Forever Advisory Council, 34
Florida Geographic Information Advisory Council, 159
Florida Governor's Council on Indian Affairs, Inc., 146
Florida Greenways and Trails Council, 34
Florida Health Access Corporation, 126
Florida High-Speed Rail Authority, 173
Florida Highway Beautification Council, 173
Florida Historical Commission, 49
Florida Housing Finance Corporation, 147
Florida Humanities Council, 50
Florida Independent Living Council, Inc., 100
Florida Inland Navigation District, 35
Florida Institute of Phosphate Research, 35
Florida Interagency Coordinating Council for Infants and Toddlers, 127
Florida Keys Aqueduct Authority, 36
Florida Legislative Committee on Intergovernmental Relations, 160

Florida Martin Luther King, Jr. Institute for Nonviolence, 101
Florida National Guard, General Officers, 160
Florida Panther Technical Advisory Council, 36
Florida Partnership for School Readiness, 67
Florida Prepaid College Board, 102
Florida Public Service Commission, 174
Florida Real Estate Appraisal Board, 67
Florida Real Estate Commission, 68
Florida Rehabilitation Council, 102
Florida Rehabilitation Council for the Blind, 147
Florida State Boxing Commission, 50
Florida State Commission on Hispanic Affairs, 148
Florida Statewide Advocacy Council, 148
Florida Transportation Commission, 174
Florida Violent Crime and Drug Control Council, 79

– G –

Gainesville-Alachua County Regional Airport Authority, 175
Govenor's Mansion Commission, 51
Governor's Advisory Council on Farmworkers Affairs, 68
Governor's Council for Young Adult Drivers, 175
Governor's Cuba Advisory Group, 161
Governor's Panel on Excellence in Long-Term Care, 127
Greater Orlando Aviation Authority, 176
Guardian Ad Litem Program Working Group, 149
Gulf of Mexico Program Citizens Advisory Committee, 37
Gulf States Marine Fisheries Commission, 37

– H –

Hamilton County Development Authority, 161
Hamilton County Memorial Hospital Board, 128
Harbor Master for Port of Fort Pierce, Saint Lucie County, 176

Hardee County Indigent Health Care Special District, 128
Health Care District of Palm Beach County, 128
Health Information Systems Council, 129
Higher Education Facilities Financing Authority, 103
Hillsborough Area Regional Transit Authority, 177
Hillsborough County Aviation Authority, 177
Hillsborough County Civil Service Board, 161
Hillsborough County Law Library Board, 51
Hospital Board of DeSoto County, 129
Housing Authorities, 149
Housing Authority, Hardee County, 150
Housing Authority, Northwest Florida Region, 150
Human Rights Advocacy Committees, 151

– I –

Immokalee Water and Sewer District, Collier County, 162
Investment Advisory Council, 162

– J –

Jackson County Hospital Corporation, 130
Jacksonville Airport Authority, 177
Jacksonville Seaport Authority, 178
Jacksonville Transportation Authority, 178
Judah P. Benjamin Memorial at Gamble Plantation Historical Site Advisory Council, 52
Judges of Compensation Claims, 86
Judicial Nominating Commissions, 87
Judicial Qualifications Commissions, 88
Jupiter Inlet District, Palm Beach County, 38
Juvenile Justice and Delinquency Prevention State Advisory Group, 80
Juvenile Welfare Board of Pinellas County, 80

– L –

Lake Shore Hospital Authority of Columbia County, 130

Land Acquisition and Facilities Advisory Board of Miami-Dade County School Board District, 103
Lawton Chiles Endowment Fund Advisory Council, 163
Learning Gateway Steering Committee, 104
Legal Affairs General Counsel, 189
Long-Term Care Ombudsman Councils, 131
Lower Florida Keys Hospital District, Monroe County, 131

– M –

Madison County Health and Hospital Board, 132
Marine Fisheries Management Councils, 38
Medicaid Pharmaceutical and Therapeutics Committee, 132
Medical Examiners Commission, 81
Merritt Island Library District Board, Brevard County, 52
Metropolitan Planning Organization of Miami-Dade County, 179
Miami River Coordinating Committee, 39
Miami-Dade County Expressway Authority, 179
Mid-Bay Bridge Authority, Okaloosa County, 180

– N –

National Conference of Commissioners on Uniform State Laws, 163
Nature-Based and Heritage Tourism Advisory Committee, 53
Nongame Wildlife Advisory Council, 39
Nonmandatory Land Reclamation Committee, 39

– O –

Office of Long-Term-Care Policy Advisory Council, 133
One Church, One Child of Florida Corporation, 151
Orlando-Orange County Expressway Authority, 180

– P –

Parole Commission, 81
Parole Qualifications Committee, 82

Partnership for School Safety and Security, 104
Pesticide Review Council, 40
Pilotage Rate Review Board, 69
Port Saint Joe Port Authority, Gulf County, 181
Practitioners Prescribing Patterns Advisory Panel, 133
Press Secretary, 188
Prison Rehabilitative Industries and Diversified Enterprises Board of Directors, 82
Public Employee Optional Retirement Program Advisory Committee, 70
Public Employees Relations Commission, 70
Public Swimming and Bathing Facilities Advisory Review Board, 133

– R –

Recycled Markets Advisory Committee, 70
Regional Marine Research Board – Gulf of Mexico, 40
Regional Planning Councils , 164
Regulatory Council of Community Association Managers, 71
Review Council for Biomedical and Social Research, 134
River Basin Boards , 41
River Water Management District Governing Boards, 43

– S –

Saint Lucie County Fire District, 164
Santa Rosa Bay Bridge Authority, 181
Sarasota-Manatee Airport Authority, 182
Secretary of the Agency for Health Care Administration, 108
Secretary of the Department of Business & Professional Regulation, 56
Secretary of the Department of Children and Families, 140
Secretary of the Department of Community Affairs, 140
Secretary of the Department of Corrections, 76
Secretary of the Department of Elder Affairs, 108
Secretary of the Department of Environmental Protection, 30
Secretary of the Department of Health , 108
Secretary of the Department of Juvenile Justice, 76
Secretary of the Department of Labor and Employment Security, 56
Secretary of the Department of Lottery, 46
Secretary of the Department of Management Services, 154
Secretary of the Department of State, 154
Secretary of the Department of Transportation, 168
Sentencing Commission, 83
Small Business Air Pollution Compliance Advisory Council, 41
South Lake County Hospital District Board of Trustees, 134
Southeast Interstate Low-Level Radioactive Waste Management Commission, 42
Southeast Volusia Hospital District, 135
Southern States Energy Board, 182
St. Lucie County Expressway and Bridge Authority, 182
State Apprenticeship Advisory Council, 105
State Apprenticeship Council Nominating committee, 72
State Board of Education, 105
State Council for Interstate Adult Offender Supervision, 83
State Emergency Response Commission, 164
State Film Commissioner, 46
State Historical Records Advisory Board, 53
State Innovation Committee, 72
State Long-Term Care Ombudsman Council, 135
State of Florida Correctional Medical Authority, 136
State Retirement Commission, 72
Statewide Drug Policy Advisory Council, 152
Statewide Nomination Commission, 88

Statewide Provider and Subscriber Assistance Program Panel, 136
Supreme Court Judgeship, 86
Supreme Court Judicial Nominating Commission, 88

– T –

Tampa Bay Commuter Rail Authority, 183
Tampa Port Authority, 183
Tampa Sports Authority, 54
Tampa-Hillsborough County Expressway Authority, 184
Taxation and Budget Reform Commission, 165
Technology Research and Development Authority, Brevard County, 73
Transportation Outreach Program (TOP) Advisory Council, 184
Tri-County Commuter Rail Authority, 185

– U –

Unemployment Appeals Commission, 73

– V –

Victims Assistance Initiative, Inc., 84

– W –

Water Advisory Panel, 42
Water Management District Governing Boards, 43
Waterfowl Advisory Council, 44
West Orange Airport Authority, 185
West Orange Healthcare District, 137
Wireless 911 Board, 165
Workers' Compensation Panel, 74

About the Author

Elizabeth McCallum is fast becoming one of the country's foremost authorities on political appointments. Through her research, interviews and experience-based observations of the appointment process, Elizabeth gives us insight into the influence-wielding world of political patronage. She enthusiastically brings her considerable knowledge to the masses and makes it easier to see how you can become part of this elite inner circle.

Elizabeth is the Principal of Baker Street Communications, a consulting firm for individuals, non-profits and companies seeking greater political insight. She has appeared as a guest speaker, panelist and workshop leader at universities, conferences and on numerous television programs.

In 1998, Elizabeth was recognized by the State of California for her work on behalf of women, when she helped establish the California Coalition for Women. Under her leadership, this coalition of prominent women's organizations conducted a project that recruited, screened and supported dozens of female candidates seeking appointment to senior level positions in California state government. Additionally, the coalition held training seminars around the state encouraging people to apply for positions on boards and commissions. In this role, Elizabeth worked with some of the most prominent women in Silicon Valley, Hollywood and in California politics.

As a regular contributor to women's magazines, Elizabeth writes articles encouraging people to vote, run for office and take an interest in shaping government policy by becoming part of the process. Elizabeth holds a bachelor's degree from Miami University in Oxford, Ohio. She and her family reside in Tampa, Florida, and have traveled extensively throughout the world, living in China, France and England.

FLORIDA CHAMBER
of Commerce

Florida's Business Advocate.

For membership information, please call 877-521-1200.

www.floridachamber.com

The Florida Guide to Political Appointments
Order Form

Order additional copies for others that may benefit from this "essential reference source for anyone who wants to get involved in Florida government"

To Place Order: Call, Fax or Mail:

Baker Street Communications
809 E. Bloomingdale Ave., Suite 409
Brandon FL 33511-8113
Phone 1-800-507-6009
Fax 813 654-1891

Or Visit our Website at: www.bakerstreetcomm.com

Date: _____
Name: _____
Business Name: _____
Shipping Address:
Street: _____
_____
City, State, Zip: _____
Phone: _____
Email: _____

Payment Information:
Check ☐
Payable to: **Baker Street Communications**
Credit Card: ☐ Type _____
Account Number: _____
Expiration Date: _____
Signature: _____
Billing Address ☐ Same as shipping
Street: _____
_____
City, State, Zip _____

Copies ____ @ $39.99 ea = _____
+ 6% Sales Tax   ($2.40 per book) _____
Sub Total _____
Shipping $5.00   5.00
+ $3.00 each additional _____
Total Order _____